Phonetic Music

with

Electronic Music

First published 1981 by

PRIMARY PRESS, Parker Ford, PA 19457
and DUSTBOOKS, Paradise, CA 95969

ISBN 0-934982-02-3 Cloth
Library of Congress Catalog Number 81-90189

Printed on acid-free paper for long time use by
Smale's Printery, Pottstown, PA 19464, United States of America

Phonetic Music

with

Electronic Music

Text by ERNEST ROBSON

Electronic Music by LARRY WENDT

Music for the hymn in *Names In the Cosmic Ocean* by STEVE RUPPENTHAL

Prosodynic Notation by MARION ROBSON

I wish to make the following acknowledgments to:

BARBARA CONNERS for the support she gave to the research on formant music and its compositions during the dark days of the 1930's.

MARION ROBSON for her indefatigable aid in countless ways without whose caligraphy the prosodynic notation could not have been developed.

JOSEPH AGNELLO, JOHN W. BLACK, GLORIA BORDEN, JANE GAITENSBY, HENRY GOEHL, PIERRE DeLATTRE, GORDON PETERSON, IRVING POLLACK, and MARTIN SCHWARTZ – I wish to acknowledge either clarification of concepts or editorial assistance or use of research facilities or the moral support of encouragement to sustain the work that led to this book. This acknowledgment is extended to many other workers in the Acoustic Society of America whose speech science papers supplied the information for developing phonetic music.

RICHARD KOSTELANETZ for prodding me to write the chapter *The Concept of Phonetic Music* and for publishing it in the magazine of aural literary criticism, **Precisely: Ten, Eleven, Twelve.**

MERROLD WROLSTED for publication of an earlier version of the discussion *Notation for Phonetic Music* in the journal, **Visible Language** 11/1975 under the title *An Orthographic Way of Writing the Prosody of English.*

JANINE CORBETT for the final editing and proofreading of this book.

Ernest Robson
September, 1981

TABLE OF CONTENTS

Upon the Electronic Realizations of Phonetic Music

In realizing the works presented here as tape pieces, one is presented with the problem of how to present essentially simultaneous acoustical events within the confines of linearly written poetic structures. These works do not deal with the complete dissolution of word-based systems like some other sound poetry might; despite their acoustical construction they retain a great deal of integrity with notable written words. Therefore to take full advantage of the techniques which a text sound composer has available to alter speech on these pieces would for the most part misrepresent what they are all about. What we have done here is to retain the clarity of the text while relying on electronic techniques to provide an acoustical underpinning and to accent particular aural-lingual events as an aid towards their differentiation.

Specific descriptions of the electronic techniques used in these realizations would take several pages and we simply do not have the space here. For the most part, I used techniques which might appear simple, obvious, and even cliche-ridden upon a first listening. This is in keeping with the quality of the texts which also appear often naive when first examined but reveal a great deal of subtlety when they are closely scrutinized. Tape pieces are meant to be played several times. Therefore it takes a little while and some close listening before these works can be completely absorbed and for their less obvious acoustical characteristics to become apparent.

In our beginning collaborations, most of the equipment which I had available to me was based around analogue magnetic tape systems. With the tape equipment I am capable of laying down around twelve tracks relatively cleanly, though I often work with twenty-four and even thirty-six on occasion. In recent years I have been able to augment this equipment with a microprocessor based digital signal processing system which I have been constructing and experimenting with. With this device I am able, among other things, to "splice" together different speech particles which exist for only about a tenth of a millisecond. I also have a variety of filter and other homemade processing equipment which I used often on these pieces. My "studio" is a converted bedroom in a twenties vintage Spanish style apartment in downtown San Jose. Most of the recordings of the voices on these tapes were done in a closet which uses books for acoustical baffling and soundproofing.

My collaborations with the Robsons have been an experiment with how to realize a written notated text as an acoustical event separate from either music or poetry. We are dealing with a vague "grey" area here that remains a vital area to examine and explore. By welding together the linguistic researches which Ernie has dealt with over the past forty or so years with contemporary speech manipulation techniques, it is hoped here to show the variety of materials and the potentials which the present day phonetic music composer has available.

Larry Wendt
San Jose
February 1, 1981

The Concept of Phonetic Music

The Concept of Phonetic Music

This treatment of speech science is written for composers of phonetic music, sound poets, song writers, writers of titles, ads, names, short dramatic dialogue and all those interested in the lyrical appeals of text written to be heard.

Phonetic music can be most clearly conceived as a somewhat special region of sound poetry. Sound poetry is any acoustic pattern of *speech* independent of grammar or meaning. It may or may not be reinforced, acoustically, by meaningful text, or instrumental music, or by environmental noise. Its physiological province is the vocal tract, even though the sounds of speech may be filtered or altered electronically. The acoustic dimensions of sound poetry are the apparent levels of frequency, amplitude, time, and silence. The apparency of these levels poses the problem of perception and recognition. Later we will deal with strategies for solving this problem.

A rich area of sound poetry is its tonal component, phonetic music. The tones of phonetic music are produced by resonances in the chambers of the mouth and throat with scalar, melodious and dissonant values. Consonants render these values more perceptible and contribute to vowel timbre. Yet the essence of the tonal information is created by amplified frequency bands of the vowels, termed "formants". Formants are the tongue shaped and volume altered resonances of the vocal tract. Although neither you nor I can speak a single formant in isolation we can hear their complex tones in vowels. We can compose formant music in different ways by selections and arrangements of vowels.

A second area of phonetic music arises from vibrations of the vocal chords. Here vibrations in the larynx create fundamental pitch, the lowest and most powerful frequency of the voice. The fundamental pitch of speech can be about 5,000 times more powerful than the oral resonances of whispers, i.e., formant tones. Yet for vowel discrimination formant patterns carry different and more detailed information than fundamental pitch. That is why birds can only sing, while people can whisper, talk, and sing. Accordingly, we may define phonetic music as the pitch patterns of sound poetry generated in the mouth and/or the vocal chords. That is what is meant by specifying phonetic music as the lyrical domain, the tonal component of sound poetry. Its dominant dimension is frequency even though its frequencies are dynamically modulated by time, intensity and silence.

An important consideration of a composer of phonetic music is to be heard. This problem is what Edgar Allen Poe long ago called the problem of a successful rendition. It lies in the uncertainty of auditory perception. This may be the most critical problem. Why?

Natural language is 90% to 95% redundant. This means about 10% of possible English carries all the language as we use it. The surplus baggage of cues which support this redundancy are acoustic and non-acoustic, the latter being semantic, grammatic, syntactic, and visual. Although vowels are the primary sources of *all tones* of English, the redundancy of English permits us to read it with no vowels at all. Consider the following two sentences. Most readers fill in the missing vowel sounds and understand the meaning of the language.

SH* *S D**NG H*R TH*NG
J*M*S W*LL DR*V* H*S R*C*NG C*R

Since phonetic music is based on vowel tones it is clear that the composer's task is to reduce, sometimes eliminate, the redundancy of contextual English. This holds for all phonetic music.

The reader may be interested to know that redundancy characterizes syllables, words, and every element and unit of contextual English. Tests show that infrequently occurring nonsense syllables generate fewer and smaller clusters of associations than do more familiar nonsense syllables. Almost twice the loudness level was needed to perceive and identify nonsense words in contrast to meaningful words located in the same place in the same sentence. The average number of recollected words spoken in isolation was 5.58. When subjects heard the same words embedded in simple whole sentences they recalled 10.5 words. In addition to the linguistic redundancies of contextual English there are phonemic constraints that curtail the information of the language. Few if any English words begin with *zt* or *wk*, or end with *jzp*.

I have been featuring the problem of redundancy in contextual English for a good reason. The 90%+ figure previously stated is enormous! When native speakers of the language read or listen to conversational English they are confronted with so many surplus cues and clues for meaning they need not nor do they pay any but a minimum amount of attention to sound patterns of speech. Therefor, composers of phonetic music who wish their pitch patterns to be heard must first eliminate the contexts of conversational English. What then are the strategies composers may utilize to maximize perception of their own pitch patterns?

There are at least six ways of reducing the redundancies of conventional English.

A writer of phonetic music may destroy contextual meaning with such excessive repetition that attention to grammar or meaning is eliminated by exhaustion of all its information. Once this elimination has occurred the residual messages are acoustic patterns of speech. Then by default no other information remains but sounds, sounds, sounds. The reader/listener becomes a sort of captive audience for the vocal values of the text. This is Gertrude Stein's hypnotic technique; a style she may have picked up as a psychology student of William James at Radcliffe College when she experimented with automatic writing, 1895-1897. The procedure is not naive. By intention, Stein introduces selected sound images and seduces the listener into appreciation of the vocal rhythms and poetic associations of Stein's peculiar speech music. The weakness of such prolonged repetitions, the crudest form of redundancy, are their wastefulness with space and paper and time.

A second strategy to make tonal patterns of speech more audible is to drastically increase the occurrence of vowels that share either high, middle, or low pitch levels. These apparent heights of pitch are formant determined. Their slopes appear on the vowel scale. *Fig. I, P. 16*

If the reader will whisper June-Joan-John-Jan-Jin-Jean the tonal rise will be heard. Reversing the order a falling tone will be heard. Whispering eliminates the more powerful vibrations from the vocal chords. On the basis of the vowel scale a verbal composer can select words for their pitch level as well as their meaning. These double screenings create a pitch vocabulary. They provide the composer with a thesaurus for a tone poem. The strategy is concentration of words with vowels on the same pitch level. An example of this tonal composition is the low toned poem, *Dirge of The Cold.* Here the low vocal components of the diphthong *ow* (*ah* as in hark blending with *oo* as in doom) appear along with the *ow* itself (towers, crowds) far more frequently than their occurrence in normal English. The increase is more than double. To reinforce the low tone of this

FIGURE I.

THE VOWEL SCALE of whisper pitches

(Notice the groupings of low, middle, and high vowels.)

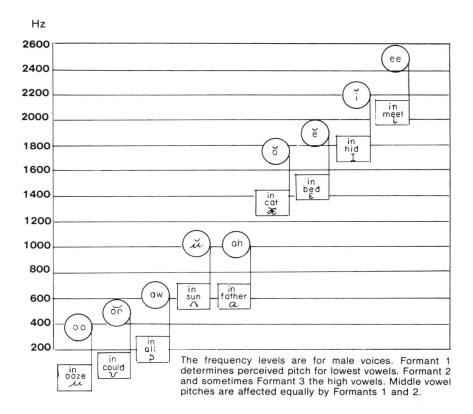

The frequency levels are for male voices. Formant 1 determines perceived pitch for lowest vowels. Formant 2 and sometimes Formant 3 the high vowels. Middle vowel pitches are affected equally by Formants 1 and 2.

This order of perceived whisper pitches has been influenced by measurements of H. L. Von Helmholtz, G. E. Peterson, H. L. Barney, I. B. Thomas, my own tests and many others.

For Spectrographic measurements of this vowel scale, see p. 106.

poem low vowels between *ah* and *oo* as *aw* (walks, war), *oh* (tolls, stones) also appear more frequently than in average English speech. Once a tone vocabulary saturates an appropriate theme, then an overcast of feeling may permeate the poem. This fusion of tonal values of words with their meaning is analogous to the song writer's selection of appropriate words for the moods in the melodic lines of the music. It is a subtle art.

Several quotations that follow are written with a prosodic notation which expresses durations of phonemes by lengths of letters; intensity by darkness or faintness of letters; pitch by the raising or lowering of vowels; pauses by lengths of blank space. Shadowings of vowels indicate modulation of pitch which adds another pitch level to the three level code. For details see *Fig. III, P. 83* and theoretical discussion of this notation, *P. 81-P. 99.*

Following is the introductory passage to *The Dirge of The Cold.*

THE DIRGE OF THE COLD

FOLLOWING LONELY CLOUDS OF SOUND

ON T⌒OW⌒EEERS   T⌒OLLS   BEELLLS

T°NGS ₀f D⌒⌒M   ON DARKENED T⌒⌒WNS

FOLLOWING MUTTERINGS ON COLD STONES OF SCUFFLED WALKS

ON CROWDS MARCHING TO THE BOOMS OF CLOCKS;

HARKING TO ROARS OF EXPLOSIONS MUFFLED IN THE RUST AND DUN

UNDER THE KINKED COMPLAINTS OF METALS ON THE STREETS,

UNDER THE SMOKELESS SMOULDERINGS IN JUNK YARDS AND THE SLUMS;

HARKING TO OPEN SHOUTS ON CONCRETE BLOCKS

REPORTING NEWS OF WARS, RUMORS OF DOOM;

DISHEARTENED WITH THE GROWLS OF ANARCHIC POWER

RULING ALL OUR TOWNS :

SORROW DROVE US TO THE NORTHERN WOODS.

Complete Composition on Pp. 72, 73, 74.

Inspection of line 2 shows the orally high vowel / Ɛ / in "bells".
Notice how "bells" is written and cued for *low fundamental*
pitch rendition which will dominate hearing of the weaker oral
tone. A reinforcement of the lowering of tone is the adjacent
/ L /. Line 7 in the passage is a high pitched phrase, "kinked
complaints of metals on the streets". This was selected for its
contrapuntal value in its low tone environment. Below is
another passage from the poem which displays some of the
rhythmic fluctuations in loon calls. Although prosodic print
cannot portray millisecond perturbations, the shape of its
rhythms can carry some descriptive, some imagistic values.

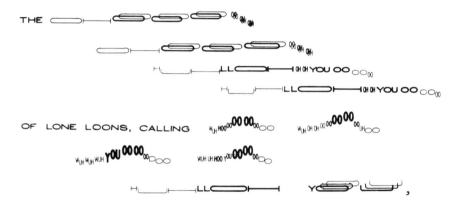

It may also be observed that the low toned vowels and
diphthongs of this poem occur so frequently they need no
notation. Only when slopes of fundamental pitch are needed for
performance or for visual values is the text notated. I mention
these fine grained techniques so the rich potential in phonetic
music may be realized. There are at least two flaws in this way of
composing. One is that the undesirable redundancy of English
is still present even though an acoustic undercoating of
consistent frequency range underlies the language. Lines of
meaningful words and sequential thoughts may dominate
attention at the expense of acoustic patterns. Then only
musically sensitive listeners will pay attention to the tonal
values. For most readers and audiences the frequency pattern of

the theme will be lost. A second disadvantage of this mode of composition is the labor time required to construct a thesaurus of tonal words.

A third strategy for perception of speech tones is to write short non-contextual English: names, titles, slogans, ads, and very short poems. The classic example of how short poetry can successfully reduce the redundancy of natural language is the 17 syllable Haiku. Once the predictabilities of conventional language are minimized, the Haiku writer can create her/his own context of imagination. Titles can create frames of reference for fitting invented words or nonsense syllables into themes, themes that guide reader/listeners towards recognizing the acoustic story of the composition. Consider the title *17 Noises in the Testicles of an Old Giant* as an introduction to dissonance.

17 NOISES IN TESTICLES OF AN OLD GIANT

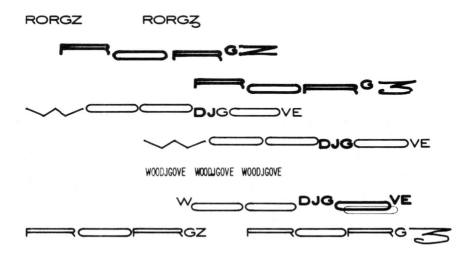

Complete Composition on P. 33.

The title, *The Evening Is Singing*, concentrates 5 tense high pitched vowels in 4 words. It is a fitting preface to vowel music that follows. The non-contextual independence of names when detached from conventional language favors perception of their formant music in *Name Suite, P. 34-42.*

TRACK 2 female

MYR^{EE}N SHA^{AH'}N · · · · · MYR^{EE}N SHA^{AH,}N

I'M MYREEN SHAHN · · · · · H^IGH MYREEN SHAHN

ON MYREEN SHAHN I'M H════GH · · · · · ⊂══⊃N₁

MYREEN SHAHN (repeated, faded out)

PASS AND GONE   PASS AND GONE (repeated)

TRACK 1 male

I'M · · · · OZZY ^{EA}ST SHINE · · · I'M GUY C^{EY}LON

I'M · · · SOLL̴Y STE[']N · · · · · I'M LEON T^OM

PART III melody (diphthong)

AH in father [ɑ] —— Ĭ in hid [I] —— I in bite [ɑ^I]

TRACK 2 female

POLL̴Y WI^INE · · · · · · POLL̴Y WI^INE

════'M POLL̴Y WI^INE

I'M H════GH · · ·ON POLL̴Y WI_INE

ON POLL̴Y WINE . . . . I'M H════GH

The same use of names occurs in parts of *Names In the Cosmic Ocean, P. 56-67.*

OO [ᵘ] ⇌ EE [ɨ]

Track 1 male & Track 2 female

TRACK 1 male

DO YOU HEAR M^USIC ════N

JUNE J^{EA}N

JUNE JEAN JUNE JEAN JUNE JEAN

J└────┘NE J════──⌃──N

A fourth strategy for making the sounds of common language more clearly perceived and more interesting is the invention of new words for their acoustic value. This procedure is over a hundred years old. It appeared in Lewis Carroll's Jabberwocky, 1855; in the multi lingual musical puns of James Joyce's "Finnegan's Wake" and in some lines of my composition *Towards Lyra and The Swan.* *See "Transwhichics", 1970, P. 23 and 24.*

The acoustic associations of Carroll's portmanteau nonsense words, Jubjub, frumious, brillig, gallumph are satirical in their context. They are consonant dependent, onomatopoeic and their semantic associations are carefully contrived. Joyce's punning nonsense words are lyrical fusions of international languages. The interests of my nonsense verbiage in *Towards Lyra and The Swan* are descriptive and thematic. Their acoustic form is an analogue of the onset-decay curves of vowels. These are rapid onsets of peaks of energy which slowly fall with time. Phrases that approximate this form of acoustic energy permeate the composition.

TOWARDS LYRA AND THE SWAN

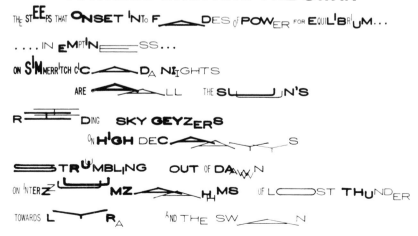

Apparently, qualities and characteristics of nonsense poetry will vary with the linguistic, technical and cultural interests of authors. Although Martin Gardner's comments on nonsense poetry in his *Annotated Alice* are scholarly, thorough and brilliant, they restrict themselves to humorous poetry. There are potentials for other attitudes and interests in nonsense language. . . not necessarily humorous at all.

A fifth strategy for preventing the delyricizing of poetry by the redundancies of contextual English is to write successions of isolated vowels for their pitch values on the vowel scale. (vowel scale, *Fig. I, P. 16)* or for their melodious or dissonant tones. Dissonance is also a form of formant "music". The illustration of dissonance that follows is from the text of *Name Suite. (bibliography 3.1) and Pp. 34 thru 42.*

TRACK 2 female

ŎŎ VŎŎLV$_A$ CRUD··Ŭ·Z^{U}LG$_A$ CHŎŎTS
Ŭ·H^{U}LD$_A$ GŎŎK··Ŭ·SUNN$_A$ GŎŎDJUK
Ŭ·LUSH WŎŎK··ŎŎ·NŎŎ₃A GUK

TRACK 1 male

ŬŬ→ŎŎ BUCKCOOK··Ŏ͝Ŏ͝Ŏ··PŎŎD STRUNGK
Ŏ͝Ŏ͝Ŏ—Ŭ·ZŎŎK SCHMUCK··ŬŬ ŎŎ BUBU ZŎŎK

Complete Composition on Pp. 34-42.

This is quite an abstract approach. It may be realized through successions of nonsense syllables as in numerous passages in *The Evening Is Singing* or again in *17 Noises in the Testicles of an Old Giant (P. 33).*

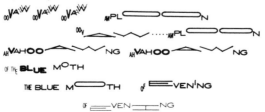

Complete Composition on Pp. 54-55.

The vowel flow is designed to carry patterns of formant qualities which interest the composer. We consider all these configurations of oral pitches as "formant music". A study of recordings of rhesus monkeys, chimpanzees and gorillas resulted in the conclusion that their vocal tracts were incapable of producing human speech. "These animals did not modify the shape of their supralaryngal vocal tracts by means of tongue maneuvers"[2.3] the way human beings do; man's tongue is less constrained. These animals do show formants spectrographically in their cries and reveal distinctive features of human speech in other utterances, yet their resonances are less flexible, less mobile and more restricted than the larger formant range of man. Man's formant music may be uniquely human. It is our "gift of tongues".

A sixth approach for establishing the perception of phonetic music is to invent *readable notation* to cue readers to speak the patterns of fundamental pitch the composer wishes them to speak. This is an important strategy for several reasons. As previously observed the fundamental pitches of the vocal chords are at least 5,000 times more powerful than the formant pitches produced by resonances in the oral chambers of the mouth. i.e., more than 35 decibels. Consequently, fundamental pitch performance dominates hearing in two situations: what is "heard" in silently reading a pitch cued text and what the audience hears during performance. With an appropriate graphic notation a composer can write visible rise/fall curves of fundamental pitch similar in shape to curves of formant pitch. (*see Fig. II, P. 24*) Live performance, then, overlays the formant melody with melody from the vocal chords. Stressed phonemes, syllables, and words carry most of the tonal information. Relative amounts of duration, intensity, and pauses contribute to stress. That is why the audilility of all pitch patterns are decisively affected by dimensions of intensity, duration, and pauses (silences). These dimensions are specified in the prosodynic notation.

Figure III, P. 83 shows an iconistic notation which generates a text that "looks like it sounds" and introduces some of the values of tone languages into English (not a different meaning with a different pitch for the same word). The justifications of phonetic music, as of all sound poetry, are its pitch and intensity levels that lie between conversation and song; and its greater durations of speech and silence than conversational speech. None of this dimensional information can be fully realized, as in music, without notation. We are dealing with poetry as a lyric art, *not* with the yak-yaks of conversation. I am convinced by experience that a notation which makes text "look like it sounds" is valuable for phonetic music in several ways. Memorability and comprehension are enhanced; rehearsals and final performance are rendered more reliably and the creation of the composition, itself, is profoundly affected.

There are other services of an alphabetic notation. It is economical. It adds a visual dimension for the recognition of the musical meaning of the text. This sometimes draws attention to the visual appearance of script as a graphic art. And it gives the script added power to express feelings and emotions. For instance, consider the sentence, "She, grieving, sat among cold rooms." Notice the down slope of its tones in *Fig. II.*

FIGURE II.

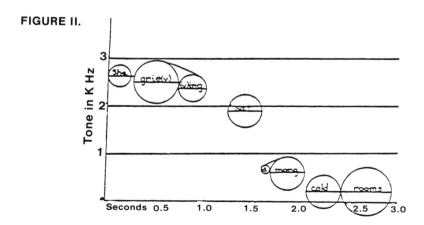

Yet a writer may present the falling tones on *Fig. II* with prosodynic notation in far less space and with equal expressiveness.

SH^E GR^{IE}V^ING SAT ᴧMONG C_OLD R⸺⸺MS

Likewise, a happier note of rising pitches appears in the diphthong melody FR_ESH SPR^ING R⸺N.
Following are the first four lines of the poem *Crows*, which demonstrate how the positive mood in the tonal rise of this phrase may become contrapuntal when preceded by three lines of low falling tones carrying a mood of depression and alarm.

CROWS

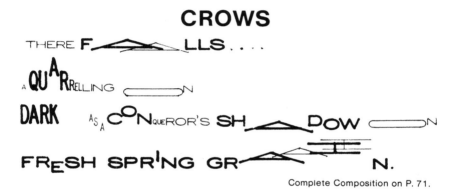

THERE F⸺LLS . . . .

^AQU^AR_{RELLING} ⸺N

DARK _{AS A}C^ON_{QUEROR'S} SH⸺DOW ⸺N

FR_ESH SPR^ING GR⸺N.

Complete Composition on P. 71.

The most interesting areas of speech music may well be its forms, the different structures of its tones. These can be generated by: scalar patterns of rising and falling vowel tones, by a variety of descriptive rhythms such as expanded onset decay curves, by tonal vectors of moods in different orders of succession, by some formant relations that are melodious in contrast to the dissonance of others. We observed that the abstract and subtle aspects of phonetic music can be clarified by association with appropriate titles, names, or short phrases. This is a mixing of different degrees of non-contextual English. Its contribution to the appreciation of phonetic music is a reminder that sounds of speech, including its tones, are embedded in the matrix of conversational speech. The new and unfamiliar contexts of phonetic music can give understanding by associating with recognizable fragments of non-contextual English.

Academicians in English departments, in semiotics, in alleged "creative writing courses," and in dramatics berate the prosodynic notation as a destruction of "ambiguity." They identify ambiguity in poetry with freedom for the reader/performer. This criticism is invalid for several reasons:

1. Poetry as a lyric art is being either eliminated or reduced to authorial individual performance. No modern instrumental music can operate without some notation. Here the vocal tract is the instrument.

2. "Ambiguity" is not distinguished from noise where noise may be confusion, mechanical defects, ignorance, or randomness masquerading as information. Nor do they distinguish between noise and ambiguity produced by information beyond the capacity of the audience, i.e., a 50,000 word vocabulary of a Shakespeare. Those who cheer for randomness should remember that death is entropy... and that the challenge of creativity is to construct new ways of imagining (ordering) existence.

3. Too much is expected from this notation; too little understood. It reveals the larger and longer rhythms and only the larger and longer rhythms of the four dimensions of sound that constitute the prosody of English speech. Because these are basic dimensions of sound they are universal. They underlie the speech of all natural languages. They do *not* cue phoneme pronunciation; nor the peculiar phase dynamics in a person's speech, nor the wide difference in range of individual voices, nor the timbre, nor the formant clarity of one individual versus another. But this notation puts more tonal information into script than anytime since the invention of rime.

Unfortunately, most academic pundits of poetry have little or no background in speech science, acoustics or information theory. With the rarest exceptions they are not creative writers of lyrics who understand the transformative feedback between composition and performance.

Relations of phonetic music to sound poetry raise a question: have sound poets produced it? They have, intuitively, sporadically. Traditionalists, too, have unconsciously incorporated tonal patterns of speech in famous lines, here and there. (*see 1.8 in the bibliography*) The service of this treatment of phonetic music is to externalize, clarify, and make available for conscious composition the information which makes speech music be what it is and what it might be. And another question: are not percussive rhythms of consonantal noise or consonantal timbre also phonetic music? They well might be. Yet, tones of speech effectively carry emotions, their rhythms are enjoyed by many, and their perceptible patterns constitute an interesting art long ignored and much neglected.

Summary

Phonetic music, the tone domain of sound poetry, may be composed in several ways with oral resonance and/or fundamental pitch of the vocal chords. For these patterns of speech to be perceived the text must reduce or eliminate the redundancies of contextual English. Then, full realization of these patterns requires notation. Rise/fall tones from the two regions of the vocal tract may assume similar rhythms of tonal change. Whether similar or dissimilar in shape, the curves of vocal chord pitch are likely to dominate hearing. However, the qualitative and descriptive values of complex formant tones may be uniquely human; and, besides serving to distinguish one vowel from another, they enable pairs and sequences of vowels to generate speech music. There is a long history of intuitive writing and performance of phonetic music by poets and other writers. Now there is a short history of its use as a conscious tool based on acoustic analysis of speech. Phonetic music is the first major increase in the information of tonal poetry since the invention of rime.

BIBLIOGRAPHY

Books

1.1 SPEECH SCIENCE PRIMER, Physiology, Acoustics, and Perceptions of Speech, **Gloria J. Borden and Katherine S. Harris,** Williams & Wilkins, Baltimore/London, 1980. A well written presentation of the necessary conditions and sufficient data for understanding speech. Most appropriate for the technical information of sound poetry.

1.2 LANGUAGE AND COMMUNICATION, George A. Miller, New York, 1951, McGraw Hill. This is the most exhaustive and intelligent study of the information of language I have read. It has influenced my thinking about language and speech.

1.3 THE MATHEMATICAL THEORY OF COMMUNICATION, Claude E. Shannon & Warren Weaver, The University of Illinois Press, 1949. This is the most influential book 1950-1970 on the statistical conception of information and redundancy. George Miller's book, 1.2, applies Shannon's measures.

1.4 EXPERIMENTAL PHONETICS: SELECTED ARTICLES, Grant Fairbanks, University of Illinois Press, Urbana, 1966. The book is valuable to sound poets for its experimental determinations of the dimensions of speech: intensity, duration, fundamental pitch; and it presents formant characteristics.

1.5 MUSIC, SOUND AND SENSATION, Fritz Winckel, New York, 1967, Dover Publications, Inc. This book includes psycho-acoustics, auditory perception, the acoustics of music, and aesthetics. It analyzes electroacoustic sound structures and gives physiological information on the behavior of listeners. A creative study.

1.6 VISIBLE SPEECH, Potter, Kopp, and Green, New York, 1947, D. Van Nostrand & Co., Inc. This is the classic presentation of the spectrographs of all the formants of all the phonemes of English. It is the largest formant thesaurus I know. It failed as a pedagogy for the deaf because it gave *too much information* for teachers and deaf students.

1.7 THE SPEECH TRAIN, The Physiology and Biology of Spoken Language, **P. B. Denes, E. M. Pinson,** Bell Telephone Laboratories, 1963. I have used this compact, accurate and clear 162 page booklet for its formant values, its consonantal features and, especially, for the excellence of the physiological explanations.

1.8 THE ORCHESTRA OF THE LANGUAGE, Ernest M. Robson, A. S. Barnes, 1959. Distributed by Primary Press. This book presents patterns of oral pitch, inherent duration, intensity, and pauses intuitively written in passages of famous writing. The first edition is out of print but it is available in library collections across the United States.

1.9 TEXT-SOUND TEXTS, an Anthology of 20th Century Sound Poetry, New York, 1980, William Morrow & Co., Inc. Edited by **Richard Kostelanetz.** A first U.S. anthology of its kind. It is comprehensive.

1.10 HISTORY OF THE DEVELOPMENT AND TECHNIQUES OF SOUND POETRY IN THE TWENTIETH CENTURY, Stephen Ruppenthal, 1975 – a thesis for the Department of Music, San Jose State University, San Jose, CA. Strong on history of continental European sound poetry. Scholarship thoughtful, interpretations interesting.

NOTE – Both 1.9 and 1.10 concern themselves with sound poetry as a total area within which phonetic music operates. Neither deals with phonetic music as such.

Technical Chap Books and Articles

2.1 ACOUSTICS OF THE SINGING VOICE, Scientific American, 3/1977 by **Johan Sundberg.** A clear contrast between the role of formants in song vs. speech. Valuable for understanding phonetic music.

2.2 AUDITORY ILLUSIONS AND CONFUSIONS, Scientific American, 12/1970 by **R. M. Warren & R. P. Warren.** Proves sloppiness of auditory perception. This implies essentiality of notation for phonetic music to become performable by diverse speakers/actors.

2.3 PRIMATE VOCALIZATION AND HUMAN LINGUISTIC ABILITY, Phillip Lieberman. Jrn. Acoustic Society of America, V. 44, No. 6, 12/1968, P. 1574. Source of comments on unique quality of phonetic music. *(P.23)*

2.4 ON REDUNDANCY OF ENGLISH:

A. *In Control Tower Language for Airplanes,* Jrn. Acoustic Society of America, V. 24, No. 6, 11/1958, P. 595, **F. C. Frick and W. H. Sumby,** the redundancy was 96%.

B. *Redundancy of Oral Monosyllabic Words in English,* **Leigh Lisker,** (SR-10, 1967) Speech Research Report of Haskins Laboratories. Redundancy was 90%.

C. *Prediction and Entropy of Printed English,* **C. E. Shannon,** The Bell Technical Jrn., V. XXX, No. 1, 1/1951. His figure was 68%.

D. *A Syllable Frequency Count,* Visible Language, V. XIV, No. 2, 1980. A qualitative suggestion of redundancy is a count of 5,000 high frequency words that occurred "more than approximately 15 times per million". These words account for 4,513,777 occurrences or 89 percent of the word tokens in 5,088,721 running words. The latter refers to running printed text where a word is defined "as a group of symbols with a space on either side." Non-verbal symbols as $, &, and graphic numbers were eliminated.

Texts for Cassettes of Phonetic Music

3.1 TEXTS FOR PHONETIC MUSIC ON ACCOMPANYING CASSETTE
Side 1

17 Noises in Testicles of an Old Giant . . . . . P. 33
Name Suite . . . . Pp. 34-42
3 Voice Arrangement of Tin Rain . . . . . . Pp. 43-44
Song of The Esopus . . . . Pp. 46-53
The Evening is Singing . . . . Pp. 54-55

Side 2

Names in The Cosmic Ocean . . . . Pp. 56-67
Voices of the Buoys . . . . Pp. 68-70

3.2 SELECTED POEMS OF ERNEST ROBSON, 1978. Spoken by **Ernest and Marion Robson.** Texts for these poems appear in *Transwhichics,* 1970, *I Only Work Here,* 1975, *Transcualisticas,* 1978... Primary Press. The compositions of phonetic music occur on the last section of the cassette.

Compositions of Phonetic Music

17 NOISES IN TESTICLES OF AN OLD GIANT

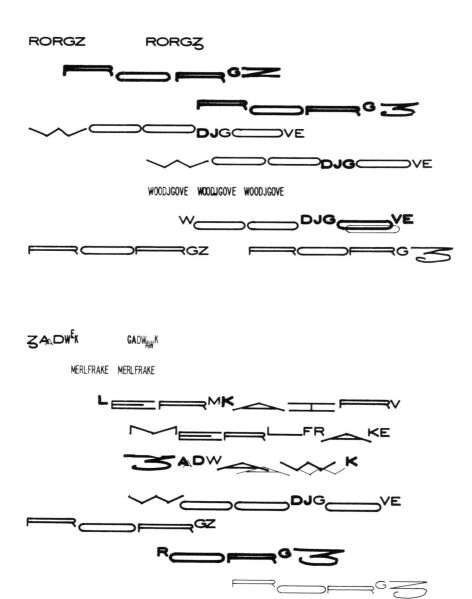

text for

NAME SUITE

by

Ernest Robson

NAME SUITE

The plain printed introductions to parts I, II, III, IV, and the close of part IV are recorded on TRACK 1, male; and TRACK 2, female. They are then recorded slightly out of sync. This gives a time lag creating an echoing of the words by the female voice.

PART 1

Her name....his name....the only consistency for idiots....
or scatterbrained persons.

PART I   melody (vowel)
o͝o in wood [ʊ] : Ĭ in hid [I]

Finale PART I

oo in boot [u] : EE in meet [i]
AH in father [a] : AW in all [ɔ] : oo in boot [u]

CHORUS OF TRACK 1 male **& TRACK 2** female

No. 1

CHORUS   RANDOM DUET male and female (TRACKS 1 & 2)

No. 2

CHORUS **RANDOM DUET OF CHORUS' 2 & 3,** sometimes single voices;
No. 3   sometimes choral (duet)

CIND^Y W^{OO}D

WOODY ROOT

DICKY SN^{OO}K

W^ILL^Y W^{OO}LF

COOK^Y H^{OO}D

CHORUS **RANDOM DUET**
No. 4   sometimes single voices; sometimes choral (duet)

L_{OO}**W^IDKN^IK**

KITTY GOOD**DIN**

N^IDW^{OO}GZ——LL

N^ICKD_{OO}**GID**IG

CHORUS **TRACK 2** female
No. 5

SPR_ING W^{OO}DS

TW_IG L^{OO}K

L_{OO}P W^INK

WOOD W——NDS

CHORUS **TRACK 1** male   **TRACK 2** female – simultaneous voices – **not random**
No. 6

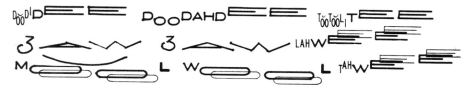

PART 2

Besides the stars and your fingerprints what other thing except your name may never change throughout your life? With any other name would Cindy Wood seem as sweet?

PART II melody (diphthong)
ε in bed [ε] —— Ĭ in hid [I] —— A in hate [ε¹]

CHORUS **TRACK 1** male **TRACK 2** female

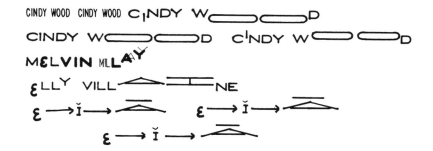

FEMALE **TRACK 2**

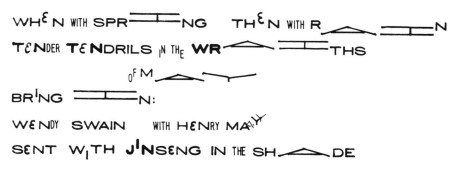

MALE **TRACK 1**

FEMALE   TRACK 2

IN DISTANT **REALMS** THEY WENT

ZENG ZING ZNE

ZENG ZING ZNE

WITH ELFIN FACES WET WITH RAIN

IN RHYTHM WITH **SELF** CENTERED SPNS

OF STRNGE TRRINS

MALE   TRACK 1

THIS ····WITH JINSENG IN THE SHDE

WITH JINSENG IN SPRING RN

MEDLEY OF TWO VOICES

MALE	FEMALE
WITH EVELYN SHAY	WITH SENLIN FRANE
WITH EDNA SAINT VINCENT MILLAY	WITH WENDY SWAIN
WITH JENNY NIMPLANE	WITH TERRY KANE
	WITH HELEN HAYES
	WITH MELVILLE SMALE

PART 3

Thou shalt not use the name of the Lord in vain. Beware! Beware! of speaking the name of Jahweh, the name of God! Open Sesame!...Open Sesame! Forgotten.....and.....Forgotten.....and Forgotten.
What price for a TV Nielsen rating of your name?

PART III   melody (diphthong)

AH in father [ɑ] —— Ĭ in hid [I] —— I in bite [ɑᴵ]

TRACK 2   female

POLLY WĪNE······POLLY WĪNE

═══'M POLLY WĪNE

I'M H═══GH···ON POLLY WIₜNE

ON POLLY WINE····I'M H═══GH

(̮ ᴜ

TRACK 1   male

CY Lᴱ ON·····Iᴵ'M CY LEON

CY LEᴼN·····I'M H═══GH ON CY LEON

CY LEON·····PASS END GⓄNE

I'M Tᴼ M DEAN Tₗᵢ NE

I'M Hᴵ GH ON   TOM   DEAN   TINE

I'M Tₒ M DEAN T═══NE

Pᴬ SS END Gₒ NE ⎤
                          repeated, blended, echoed
TOM DEAN TINE ⎦

TRACK 2 female

MYR^{EE}N SHA^{HH}N·····MYR^{EE}N SHA_{HH}N

I'M MYREEN SHAHN·····H^IGH MYREEN SHAHN

ON MYREEN SHAHN I'M H━━GH·····⬭N:

MYREEN SHAHN (repeated, faded out)

PASS AND GONE   PASS AND GONE (repeated)

CHORUS TRACK 1 male   **TRACK 2** female

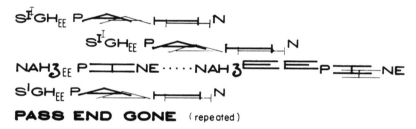

PASS END GONE (repeated)

TRACK 2 female

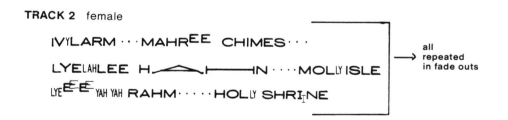

→ all repeated in fade outs

TRACK 1 male

I'M····OZZY ^{EA}ST SHINE···I'M GUY C^{EY}LON

I'M···SOL_{LY} ST^EI N·····I'M LEON T^OM

Would a social security number for your name as B 222 – C 22 – G 2222......
make you feel a bit distinctive?
Where are the names of the poets under the rubble of the city of Ur? Where are
the names of the persons who invented the barbed wire fence... or the
heterodyne tube? Who discovered the wheel?

PART IV dissonances (vowel)

Ŭ in sun [ʌ] : ŏŏ in wood [ʊ] : OH in boat [O]

CHORUS TRACK 1 male **TRACK 2** female

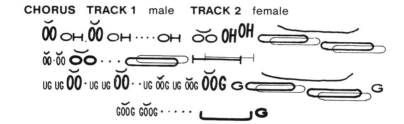

TRACK 1 male

OŏCH OH3 ··OŏCH OH3 ᴴᵁᴴᵁᴴᵁ H⊂══⊃△K SHMUK
OŏK OAK ··OŏK OAK ·····SCH⊂══⊃⊂══⊃LTZE
                                        OATS

TRACK 2 female

SCHŏŏLTZE **MUST** G⊂══⊃

SHMUCK SHOUL**D** G⊂══⊃

CHORUS TRACK 1 male **TRACK 2** female

Ŭ⟶ŏŏ⟶OH   Ŭ⟶ŏŏ⟶OH

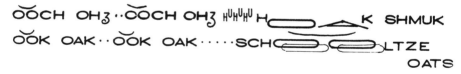

B⊂══⊃TH BOTH BOTH B⊂══⊃TH

Pᴬss END GₒNE

TRACK 2 female

OŎ VŎŎLV_A CRUD··Ŭ·Z^ULG_A CHŎŎTS

Ŭ·H^ULD_A GŎŎK··Ŭ·SUNN_A GŎŎDJUK

Ŭ·LUSH WŎŎK··OŎ·NŎŎƷ_A GUK

TRACK 1 male

ŬŬ —OŎ BUCKCOOK ··ŎŎ ŎŎ·· PŎŎD STRUNGK

ŎŎ ŎŎ— Ŭ·ZŎŎK SCHMUCK··ŬŬ OŎ BUBU ZŎŎK

TRACK 2 female

MOE **D** 3

ROHN_A **RŎŎTCH**

TRACK 1 male

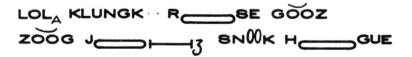

LOL_A KLUNGK·· R SE GŎŎZ

ZŎŎG J 3 SNꝊK H GUE

CHORUS   TRACK 1   male   **TRACK 2**   female

ŎŎ Ŭ··ŎŎ Ŭ·· G G SHMUK··ŎŎ OH··ŎŎ OH SHŎŎLTZ OATS

What is more superficial than a name   NOT SO! He who steals my purse steals trash! But he – she who sullies my good name buries me in the garbage dumps of history... and pollutes my image forever......forever.

The vowels and diphthongs that appear before stanzas are formant related. They are discussed in *Formant Music in Vowel and Diphthong Tones*, P. 101 thru P. 127.

TIN RAIN

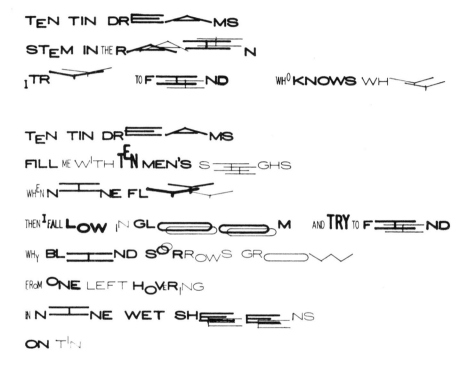

TIN RAIN

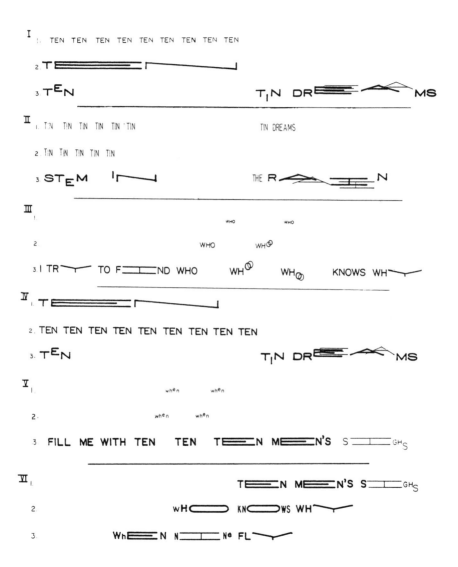

This arrangement was written by **DAVID ROTH.**

VII

1. why

2.

3. THEN FALL LOW IN GLOOM

VIII

1. WHY

2. WHY

3. AND TRY   TO FIND   WHY BL⸺ND SORROWS GROW

IX

1. ◯NE

2. ◯NE

3. FROM ◯NE   LEFT HOVERING   IN

X

1. NINE NINE NINE NINE NINE NINE NINE NINE NINE

2. N⸺⸺⸺e

3. NINE   WET SH⸺NS

XI

1.

2.

3. ◯N TIN

SONG OF THE ESOPUS

Electronic Music by
LARRY WENDT

Text by
ERNEST ROBSON

SONG OF THE ESOPUS

PRELUDE TO SECTION I

A melody is introduced, mixed with continuous murmurings of a mountain brook; followed by staccato noises; ending with soft burblings of a brook.

SECTION I

TRACK I = male　　**TRACK II** = female　　**TRACK III** = music

TRACK III　Background to the oral renditions of the poetry consists of soft sounds of murmuring waters.

TRACK II　female

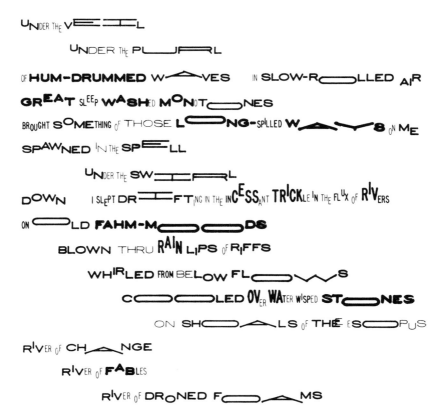

UNDER THE VEIL

UNDER THE PLURAL

OF **HUM-DRUMMED** WAVES　IN SLOW-ROLLED AIR

GREAT SLEEP WASHED MONOTONES

BROUGHT SOMETHING OF THOSE LONG-SPILLED WAYS ON ME

SPAWNED IN THE SPELL

UNDER THE SWIRL

DOWN　I SLEPT DRIFTING IN THE INCESSANT TRICKLE IN THE FLUX OF RIVERS

ON OLD **FAHM-MOODS**

BLOWN THRU RAIN LIPS OF RIFFS

WHIRLED FROM BELOW FLOWS

COOLED OVER WATER WISPED STONES

ON SHOALS OF THE ESOPUS

RIVER OF CHANGE

RIVER OF **FABLES**

RIVER OF DRONED FOAMS

TRACK I   male

TRACK I & TRACK II   male and female

TRACK III   music   ± sound effects similar to those in the introduction. The last part of this music changes into an introduction to Section II.

SONG OF THE ESOPUS

PRELUDE TO SECTION II

Again mountain brook sounds of falling waters, but this time dominated by the melody of a 24 oscillator induced refrain, the same melody that faintly sounded through the Prelude to Section I.

SECTION II

TRACK III   Background of soft sounds of murmuring waters.

TRACK II   female

THERE LISPS IN TURNED EDDIES

WERE STONE-THROWN-ECHOES OF THE EARTH'S EDGES

CHURNING THEIR REVERBERANT DIRGE OF EROSION

MURMURING OF SHORN STONE

BOWLS SHADOWS HOLLOWED FORMS

STORM-HEWN URNS FULL OF LOW TONES

TRACK I   male

STORM-HEWN URNS FULL OF LOW TONES

TRACK II   female

MURMURING OF MOWING THE WORLD'S CURVED SURFACE

ITS DROPPED CREEKS WITH ITS CUT-PEAKS GETTING CALAMITY ECHOES

SLOUGHED STILLED SLOW-TOWED SMOOTHED

BY THE STEADY LEVELING OCEAN'S PULL

THERE I LEARNED

THE TARE THE WEAR OF EARTH'S TERRACES

MAY BE MEASURED WITH THE MEADOW'S DEPTH IN LOAM

TRACK I   male

TRACK I AND TRACK II   chorus

PAUSE HERE

TRACK I AND TRACK II   chorus

THERE ST**O**NE-THROWN-E**CH**O**E**S   OF TH**E** E**A**RTH'S E**DG**E**S**
CH**U**R**N**ING THEIR R**E**V**E**R**B**E**R**ANT **DIRGE**   OF ER**O**S**ION**

TRACK III   music Suitable river noise and music compatible with introducing music/noise.

50

SONG OF THE ESOPUS

PRELUDE TO SECTION III

Same melodic refrain superimposed on watery murmurings, increasing in volume against a background of digitally spliced voices of peoples.

SECTION III

TRACK III   Background: First a faint murmuring of brook waters, later quite noisy; a variety of sounds of speech mixed with water sounds.

TRACK I   male

AMONG PERCUSSIONS ECHOED THRU THE BONES

AND LULLED BY TIME

TRACK II   female

THE EARTH'S WEAR   DREW ME THRU

DREW ME DOWN UNDER DISTILLED CURTAINS   OF THE ANCIENT RAINS

UNDER THE FALL

TRACK I   male

UNDER THE FALL

THE LONG POUR

UNDER MOUNTAINS SLABS TOMBS

MONUMENTS OF SLOW CHANGE

DREW ME THRU SHADOWS OF THEIR FAULTS AND FLAWS

TRACK II   female, whispered

THERE I HEARD THE VOICE OF PEOPLES

AH OO EE OO AW EE

TRACK I   male, normal loudness

TH^{ER}E I H_{EA}RD TH_E V^{OI}CE OF P PLES

AH   OO   EE   OO   AW   EE

TRACK II   female, with great clarity

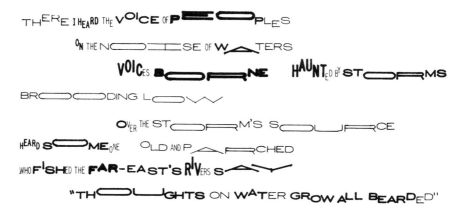

TRACK I   male

"TH GHTS ON WATER GROW ALL BEARDED"

FINALE

TRACK III   Melodic refrain recapitulated but broken up with jagged staccato and random noises suggesting animal cries.

Technical Explique

1. *Water Sounds:* 2 superimpositions of a recorded stream slightly out of phase.

2. *River Music:* 4 superimpositions of 6 square wave oscillators of the same melodic line slightly altered in pitch in a computer controlled random fashion.

3. *"Incessant Trickles":* 4 superimpositions with different reverberant filtered qualities of the word "thoughts" taken from the recorded male reading of "thoughts"... as processed by a computer. Parts of the spoken word are played back at different speeds.

4. *"The Voice of Peoples":* The female reading in Section I was passed through a digital gate; the resultant sound was processed through a variable band pass filter; next passed to two tape recorders with a single tape threaded between them. This repeats the sounds and produces some long echo effects.

5. *Termination With Old Man Cackles:* generated like (1) above. The whole spoken word is "played back" at different data rates. A higher frequency band pass filter was used.

The Song of The Esopus is not "pure" phonetic music in the technical sense of the term. Its acoustic character was determined by the phonemic scanning system specified in *The Orchestra of the Language*. Nevertheless, it is included in this section because of its tonal lines, its watery rhythms and its electronic music.

THE EVENING IS SINGING

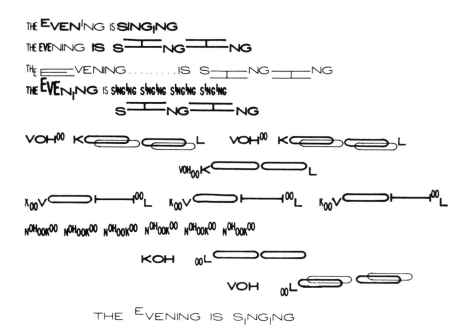

PLoongaw VEEn PLoongaw VEEn PLoongaw VEEn PLoongaw VEEn

PL⬭⬭ONGaw V⬭EE⬭N

⬭NGN⬭⬭FRaw R⬭NG

⬭NGN⬭⬭FRaw R⬭NG

ooVAIW ooVAIW ooVAIW AWPL⬭⬭N

ooV AW⬭⬭⬭AWPL⬭⬭N

AH VAHOO A WNG AH VAHOO A WNG

OF THE BLUE MOTH THE BLUE MOTH THE BLUE MOTH

WEMMyLETT⬭NG SHE'S TELLING M⬭

OF THE BLUE MOTH THE BLUE MOTH

THE BLUE M⬭TH of ⬭VENING

OF ⬭VEN⬭NG

NEMMyLET NEMMyLET NEMMyLET NEMMyLET NEMM⬭⬭LETT⬭NG

THE WAY SHE IS SAYing

"THE EVNING IS SINGING"

THE EVENING⬭S SINGING

NEMMyLETT⬭NG WHEN SHE TELLS M⬭

THE EVNING IS SINGING

THE EVENING⬭S SINGING

SINGING SINGING SINGING SINGING

S⬭NG⬭NG

S⬭NG⬭NG

NAMES IN THE COSMIC OCEAN

text by
ERNEST ROBSON

prosodynic print by
MARION ROBSON

music by
STEVE RUPPENTHAL

technical realization by
LARRY WENDT

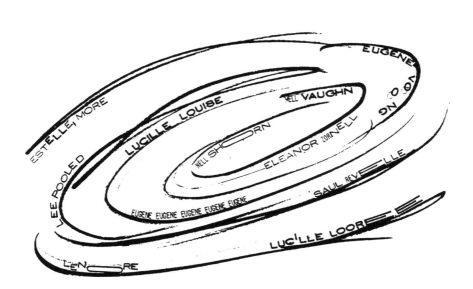

NAMES IN THE COSMIC OCEAN
a satire of cosmic nonsense with phonetic music

Background of bull frog croaks and a foreshadow of the last refrain

Track
4

WOMAN COSMOLOGIST
Names in the Cosmic Ocean under the auspices of SORTU, the society of our reactions to the Universe. Text by Ernest Robson, Technical realization by Larry Wendt, music by Steve Ruppenthal.
CHARACTERS
Harmonious Name Society
Discordant Name Society
Master of Ceremonies
Woman Cosmologist
Critical Astronomer
Mathematician
Christian chorus and Buddhist chant
Recorded at Frog Hollow Studio, December 1978 and February 1979 (and revised July 1979)

Track
3

(CHORUS BACKGROUND)
Whispered: "memories, memories of the lost Lenore"
Spoken: "Memories of the lost Lenore"
(n.b. Formant music in "Lenore" from vowels
or / $\mathcal{E}$: $\mathfrak{I}$ / pervades the final movement of this composition. It was first recognized and developed by Edgar Allen Poe in his use of "nevermore" as a refrain in his poem, *The Raven.* See Poe's *Philosophy of Composition.*)

Track
3

MASTER OF CEREMONIES
Greetings from Sortu, Sortu the society of our reactions to our Universe and **the** Universe. Sortu, the society that tells us where we are, where we'll be in the Cosmos. . . because of what, why, when we become cosmic coined, cosmic cribbed, cosmic cloned. (pause)   By the double star in the Big Bear; by the illuminated condom from Sears Roebuck in the Teapot; by the creation of hydrogen out of nothing in empty space; by the probability measures of the singularity of our Cosmos I convene the first convocation of Sortu and call on THE HARMONIOUS NAME SOCIETY.

Track
1
male
&
Track
2
female

OO[ᵁ] ⇌ EE[ᶥ]

TRACK 1   male

DO YOU HEAR MᵁSIC ═══N

JUNE JᴱAₙ

JUNE JEAN JUNE JEAN JUNE JEAN

J└──┘NE J═══⟨───⟩N

TRACK 2 female

LUC^I~I~LLE LOOREE   LUC^I~I~LLE LOOREE

LOOR^EE LOOR^EE LOOR^EE

LUC^ILLE LOOR⬛⬛ ⬛⬛   (echoed fade outs)

TRACK 1 male

DEAN R^OO N·· DEAN R^OO N·· DEAN R^OO N (fade out)

EU GENE EU GENE EU GENE (pause)

EU GENE LOOR^EE ..... EU GENE LOOR^EE

EUGENE LOOR^EE (fade out)

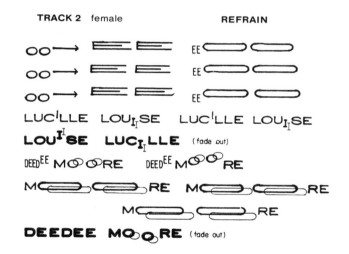

TRACK 2 female   **REFRAIN**

LUC^ILLE LOU_I~I~SE   LUC^ILLE LOU_I~I~SE

LOU^I~I~SE LUC_I~I~LLE (fade out)

DEED^EE MⵔⵔRE   DEED^EE MⵔⵔRE

M◯◯RE M◯◯RE

M◯◯RE

DEEDEE MO₀RE (fade out)

TRACK 1 male

LEE POOLED   LEE POOLED

L^EE P◯◯LED

R^U BIE VOORH^EE Z   **RUBIE VOORH^EE Z** (echoed)

EU GENE EU GENE EU GENE EU GENE EU GENE EUGENE V◯◯NG

EUGENE VO₀NG

Track

male

&

Track 2 female

CHORUS
TRACK 1 male **& TRACK 2** female

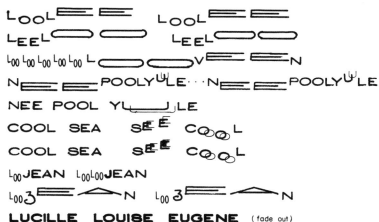

LUCILLE LOUISE EUGENE (fade out)

FORMANT FREQUENCY RELATIONS IN THE
PHONETIC MUSIC OF THIS COMPOSITION.

VOWEL	DOMINANT	RECESSIVE
oo in boot (ᴜ)	F₁ 375 Hz	F₂ 825 Hz
EE in meet (ɪ)	F₁ 2,500 Hz	F₂ 360 Hz

Track 3

MASTER OF CEREMONIES
Does the Astronomer or the Cosmologist on our panel care to comment?

Track 4

WOMAN COSMOLOGIST
Their Universe seems to be their names.

Track 1 & Track 2 (chorus)

"When they **sing** with their names
They sing **with** themselves.
When they sing **of** themselves
They sing **with** their names.
Since **they. . . . . themselves**
Are their Universe. . . . .
Since they are **their Universe**
Their Names **praise** their Universe."

Track 4

WOMAN COSMOLOGIST
"Their Universe seems to be their names.
Their Universe seems to be their names.
Their Universe seems to be their names." (fade out)

Track 3

MASTER OF CEREMONIES
"Now by the X-ray hairs around the black hole of the Swan –
Let us listen to the Discordant Name Society"

Track
1
male
&
Track
2
female

DUET

Ă as in cat [æ] ⇆ Ĕ as in red [ɛ]

MALE   TRACK 1

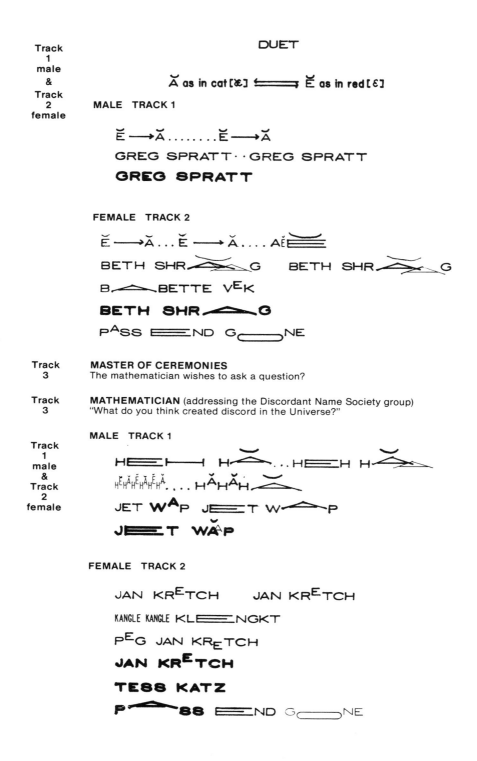

Ĕ⟶Ă.......Ĕ⟶Ă

GREG SPRATT··GREG SPRATT

GREG SPRATT

FEMALE   TRACK 2

Ĕ⟶Ă...Ĕ⟶Ă....Aĕ

BETH SHR⟋⟍G   BETH SHR⟋⟍G

B⟋⟍BETTE Vᴱᴷ

BETH SHR⟋⟍G

PᴬSS ══ND G══NE

Track
3

MASTER OF CEREMONIES
The mathematician wishes to ask a question?

Track
3

MATHEMATICIAN (addressing the Discordant Name Society group)
"What do you think created discord in the Universe?"

MALE   TRACK 1

Track
1
male
&
Track
2
female

Hᴱ⊢⊣ H⟋⟍...Hᴱ⊢H H⟋⟍

Hᴱ𝐻Ăᴱ𝐻Ăᴱ𝐻Ăᴱ𝐻Ă....HĂHĂH⟋⟍

JET WᴬP J══T W⟋⟍P

J══T WĂP

FEMALE   TRACK 2

JAN KRᴱTCH   JAN KRᴱTCH

KANGLE KANGLE KL══NGKT

PᴱG JAN KRᴱTCH

JAN KRᴱTCH

TESS KATZ

P⟋⟍SS ══ND G══NE

60

MALE TRACK 1

ᴷᴬᴺᴳᴸᴱ ᴷᴬᴺᴳᴸᴱ KL^{E}NGKT

FR$_A$K ZELCH   FR$_A$K ZELCH

FRAK ZELCH

CHORUS MALE AND FEMALE TRACKS 1 & 2

ᴬꜰꝼ ᴬꝼꝼ ^{E}TH. . . . . . .SCHRAFF AZM^{E}TH

Ĕ ⟶ Ĕ ⟶ A$^△$ WEST TEX PR$^△$TT

ₕᴬ̆ₕᴱ̆ᴴₕᴱ̆ᴴ **MANDEL KR^{Ē}PS**. . . . .A$_\wedge$ND

CLARENCE GR^{E}TCH. . . . .A$^△$ND

FRAN BETH V^{E}K. . . .

⟋⟍ND ₕᴱᴴₕᴱᴴₕH ⟋⟍   B═══GETS

═══DSE═══L KR^{A}P. . .═══DSEL KR^{A}P

═══DSEL KR^{A}P

FORMANT FREQUENCIES NOT SHARED IN DISSONANT
PAIRS OF VOWELS THROUGH THIS PASSAGE

Ă[æ] as in cat ⟷	Ĕ[ɛ] as in red
F_1 835 Hz	F_1 610 Hz
F_2 1750 Hz*	F_2 1900 Hz

*The F_2 frequency of Ă[æ] is so irregular it ambiguates
tonal perception especially in the neighborhood of
other vowel formants that may overlap.

MASTER OF CEREMONIES
"By the Kalpa of Aeons of exploding galaxies; the ignitions of supernova. . . . .
and by the Karma of stars. . . . .reborn out of hydrogen clouds and the dust and
debris of dead suns, let the Buddhists on the breath of Brahma throughout the
Cosmos. . . . .tell us of our Universe.

Musical background leading to. . . . . .

Track   **BUDDHIST CHANT**
4

Stanza #1.....repeat 3 times

BOOD DAHN KAHR MAHN VAHN JIN JAHNG REEN

Stanza #2.....repeat 3 times

VOHD GAWN TUNG TAHN JEN JING VAME KEEN
KEEN VAME JING JEN TAHN TUNG GAWN VOHD

Stanza #3.....repeat 3 times

VOHL KAWNG BUNG DAHDAH JIM GIN BANE
BANE JIN JAHR DAHDAH BUNG KAWNG VOHL

Stanza #4.....repeat 3 times

JEEN DANE MING TUNG KAHN PAWNG BAWNG DOME
DOME BAWNG PAWNG KAHN TUNG MING DANE JEEN

Stanza #5.....repeat 3 times

KEENG MANE MING JIN JAHR GAWN TUNG TOME
TOME KAWNG DUN BAHNG JIN BANE ZING ZEEN

Track   **WOMAN COSMOLOGIST**
4   "What **was** your message about Nirvana and Karma?" Please repeat

Track   **Repeat Buddhist chant**
4

BOOD DAHN KAHR MAHN JIN JAHN REEN
BOOD DAHN KAHR MAHN JIN JAHN REEN
BOOD DAHN KAHR MAHN JIN JAHN REEN

Track   **MATHEMATICIAN**
3   "Redundancy has no limits."

Track   **CRITICAL ASTRONOMER**
3   "And so has Cosmic nonsense."
                (these statements are repeated....then a third "Redundancy has
                no limits" leads into....)

Track   **MASTER OF CEREMONIES**
3   "By the Holy Ghost in the black hole; by the Virgin Mary in the white star Spica;
      by the rebirth of light from Jesus rekindled in comets out of debris from the
      planet that exploded....give us enlightenment about the universe....you
      God fearing Christians."

GENESIS HYMN

I'm the spirit of God
that moved within the waters
I am the Power that brought
the Light out of void and darkness.

It is I who called Light. . ."DAY"
and "Night". . .the name of darkness.
I **am** the master who made
the moons and stars and planets

I said "Let Galaxies be
the burning cities of the night;
Let life arise on Earth
And Man be made in my image."

Let energy be Eternal.
I'm the power in all things.
Obey me, the Source of Power
In all forms of the Cosmos.

WOMAN COSMOLOGIST
"Since you passive, impersonal Buddhists cannot or will not reconcile your
Nature Gods with the power obsessed God of the Christians/Hebrews let us
become enlightened by the vision of the Cosmosaic Name Society who claim
their forefathers made our Human Universe.

CRITICAL ASTRONOMER
    Chants:
        Cosmosaic Name Society
        Cosmosaic Name Society
        Cosmosaic Name Society
        What kind of Cosmic nonsense is this?

MASTER OF CEREMONIES
I am Jesus J. Einstein Karl Marx Christ;. . . Darwin Friederich Engels
Zoroaster Freud;. . . Clark Maxwell, Mohammed, Moses, Max Planck;. . .
Archimedes Columbus, Isaac Newton, Mao Tze Tung;. . . Tito, Pope Pi ass, Pi
ass, Pi ass, Pi ass, Pi ass, Watson, Crick;. . . Thomas Jefferson, Lenin. Julius
Caesar, Genghis Khan;. . . Aristotle, Aristarchus, George Reimann, Tycho
Brahe;. . . Copernicus, Pasteur, Emmanuel Kant, Baudelaire;. . . Pablo Picas-
so, Edgar Poe and Li Po and Galileo;. . . and I am Johann Bach, John von
Neumann, Jonathan Swift, Johnny Appleseed, Johann Kepler, John Baptiste
Poquelin Moliere – and Sir John **of** the john;. . . Dr. Harvey, Babe Ruth and
the Virgin Mary;. . . Shakespeare, Charlemagne and Lobachevski;. . . Charlie
Chaplin, Charles de Gaul, Robson, Wendt and Ruppenthal.

FEMALE VOICE
What they did was. . . . and **IS** and will **BE**. . . . in **ME**
What **IS**. . . . in **ME**
IS. . . . what they **DID**

(instructions, technical – very, very quietly some frogs noises accompany
the above. . . .this is a **prelude** to later frog chorals)

GENESIS HYMN

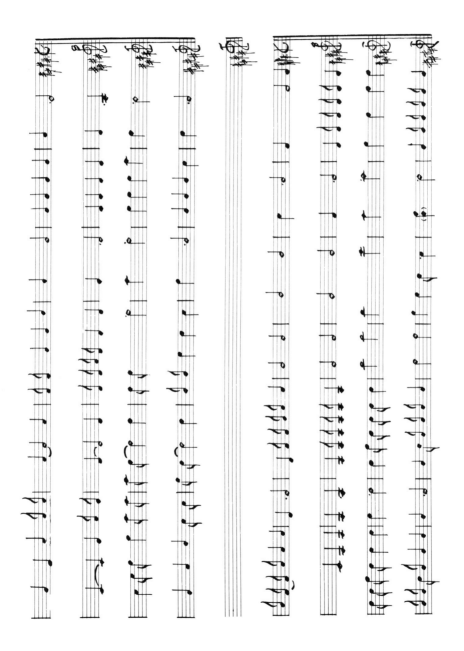

Track 3

CRITICAL ASTRONOMER

Those are not Cosmosaic names. They are. . .human Universe names. The human Universe is to the Cosmos less than a frog pond to the seven seas, less than a frog pond to the seven seas.

(**note:** Here the frog pond domain of the Human Universe is compared with the great Cosmos of boundless Space/Time. It is **characterized tonally** by different frogs and frog choruses that accompany but **do not** garble the speech or meanings of the recordings. Low pitched, primitive Columbian whistles may also accompany. . . and bullfrog-like syllables are uttered by a male voice.)

Track 1

MALE VOICE – BULLFROG

mixed with or accompanied by real frog chorals. The cue is the frog pond metaphor.

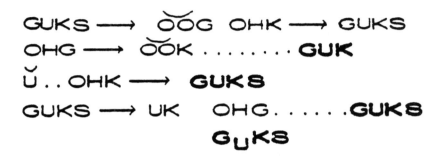

Track 3

MATHEMATICIAN

The leaders of our earthly Universe could **not** know. . . everything. . . They're **not** omniscient. . . .but we have **got** ignition. . . . . . .that's **it.** We've got ignition . . . I guess that's it. . . .or we **did** have.

Track 4

WOMAN COSMOLOGIST

In spite of their ignitions, the heroes of human history, the harmonious, the discordant, the Buddhists, the Christian societies all failed to make us feel at home in the Universe without Cosmic Nonsense.

Track 3

MATHEMATICIAN

But we have got ignition. . . I guess that's it. (fade out frog chorus)

Track 3

MASTER OF CEREMONIES

"By the music of planets in the numbers of Kepler on the faces of regular polyhedra – surely you astronomers who have landed men on the moon; who so precisely predict the paths and brightness of comets (except for comet Kohoutec which lost its tail over a piece of its head) yet you who have enlarged our Universe by billions of light years during the 20th century. . . . .surely you can make us feel at home in the Universe. . . . .without **Cosmic Nonsense.**

Track 3

MATHEMATICIAN

Maybe we better define Cosmic Nonsense before we make statements.

| Track 4 | **WOMAN ASTRONOMER**
Yes, Cosmic Nonsense is any model of the Universe that claims to be final and exhaustive. |

| Track 3 | **CRITICAL ASTRONOMER**
Garbled talk
Agreed!! But. . .if the Universe was originally elementary particles in the first place, **what** put them there? Where did they come from? Which model can tell us this? What cosmic model can account for the existence of mass/energy or matter in the Universe? We know **very** little about the large scale distribution of matter in space. We don't know whether continuous creation is going on. . .or will continue. We do **not** know **over what range** of space and time the constants of astrophysics **are** constant. We do **not** know if our Universe is singular, or – if not – there are more universes than we can dream of. **Our** models are more sophisticated forms of Cosmic Nonsense. . . .as you define it. |

| Track 3 | **MATHEMATICIAN**
We are not omniscient. . . .but we have got ignition. . . . .that's it!
We are not omniscient. . . .but we have got ignition. . . . .that's it!
We are not omniscient. . . .but we have got ignition. . . . .that's it! |

| Track 3 | **CRITICAL ASTRONOMER**
How modest. . . . .this Cosmic Nonsense. |

| Track 3 | **MATHEMATICIAN**
The challenge to create a final and exhaustive model of the Universe inspired Kepler, Newton, Einstein and all cosmologists. This challenge expanded the boundaries of human knowledge. That's the value of **our** kind of Cosmic Nonsense. |

| Track 4 | **WOMAN ASTRONOMER**
Since one of the few things about this Cosmos we surely do know is its many forms of energy let us listen to the acoustic waves of our music as an expression of the whole Universe. |

| Track 1 & Track 2 male & female | **MUSICAL INTRODUCTION to**

e./ ε / --- aw/ $\mathfrak{I}$ /   name suite ending in "Memories of the lost Lenore."
The final fade out of the refrain "Memories of the lost Lenore." |

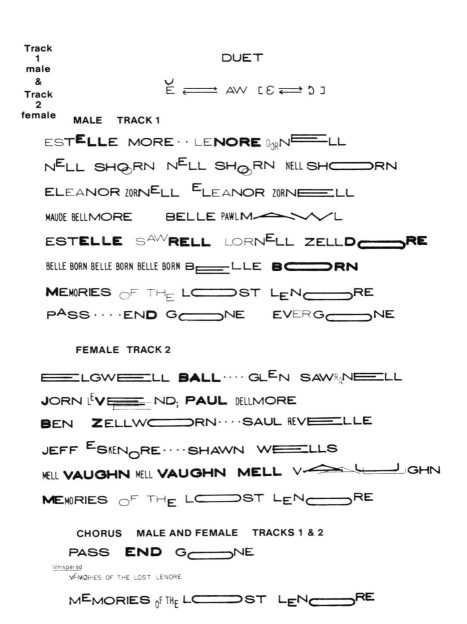

FORMANT FREQUENCY RELATIONS IN THE
PHONETIC MUSIC OF THIS COMPOSITION.

VOWEL	DOMINANT	RECESSIVE
aw in all (ɔ)	F_1 625	F_2 850
ĕ in bed (ɛ)	F_2 1900	F_1 610

VOICES OF THE BUOYS

Prelude: Sounds of waves of the sea mingled with distant chimings and occasional fog warnings.

TIGHTLY TIED AS IF WIRED

TO A SOLID BOTTOM

SWAYING WITH THE WAVES

REPEATING THE BEATS OF THE DEEPS

THE NOISE OF THE TIRELESSLY TOSSING BUOYS

UNCOILS ON A SEA WIDENING OF HORIZON

THE TONGED RECOILS OF THE NOISE OF THE BUOYS

DRAWN WITH THE LONG CLONG

THAT IRON HAWSERS HAWL

ARE ALWAYS CALLING

ALWAYS CALLING

HOW THIS RISING FALLING

STAYS STABLY BASED UPON AN UNCHANGED ORIGIN

BENEATH THE SWEEPS

IT SEEMS TO BE A LEAN AND MINERAL TREE
RECOILING FROM THE BOYANT WHORLS OF SALTY WATER
IN THE DAWNS BENEATH THE SEA
A SIDE WISE LEANING AND A LOLL
WHOSE WINNOWING SEEMS UNWEIREDLY TO BE REVEALING
BLUE WINDS KEELING
THRU THE INTERIOR IN THE SPHERED MARINE
YET THESE UNWEIRED CLONGINGS
WHEN IN PERIOD PEELINGS
THESE TURQUOISE NOISES OF THE BUOYS
LOITER ON IN SPITE OF LOST SPAWN
IN SPITE OF ALL THE LOST OIL WASTED ON THE BAY
IN SPITE OF CRIMES WARS WRONGS
THE CRIES SNORTS
TOSSED BODIES OF BLEEDING SEAMEN
DESTROYED IN THE DEEPS
STILL THE BUOYS ARE ALWAYS BUOYANT

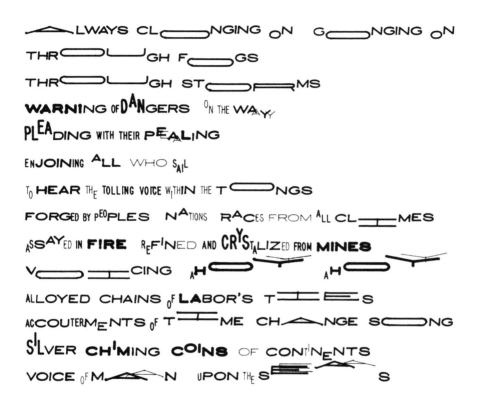

Finale: Recapitulation of the sounds in the prelude and background.

CROWS

THERE F A LLS . . . .

A QU A RRELLING O N

DARK AS A CON QUEROR'S SH A DOW O N

FRESH SPRING GR A N.

THERE'S A D A RKNESS

ON A BLACK-FL A PPED DARK NESS

ON THE J O NQUIL S U N.

TH A T QUAR RELLING . . . . . .

AND TH A T D A RKNESS

CALL A WAR NING

FOR A LL

ITS THE SW AR TNESS B RA SH NESS H OO K-PECKED B O LD NESS

IN THE H AR SH C A WW S OF ROOKS

S A FE LY P ER CH ED

ON W OO D EN SHOUL DER S OF OA KS . . . .

CH A T TER ING . . . . . . A N GRIL Y . . . . . .

A T THEIR E N E M Y

THE H A W K

OR F O X

THE DIRGE OF THE COLD

FOLLOWING LONELY CLOUDS OF SOUND

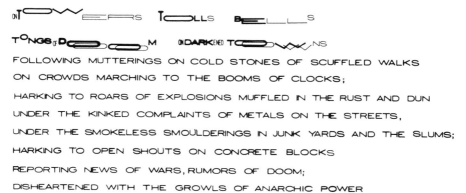

FOLLOWING MUTTERINGS ON COLD STONES OF SCUFFLED WALKS
ON CROWDS MARCHING TO THE BOOMS OF CLOCKS;
HARKING TO ROARS OF EXPLOSIONS MUFFLED IN THE RUST AND DUN
UNDER THE KINKED COMPLAINTS OF METALS ON THE STREETS,
UNDER THE SMOKELESS SMOULDERINGS IN JUNK YARDS AND THE SLUMS;
HARKING TO OPEN SHOUTS ON CONCRETE BLOCKS
REPORTING NEWS OF WARS, RUMORS OF DOOM;
DISHEARTENED WITH THE GROWLS OF ANARCHIC POWER
RULING ALL OUR TOWNS:
SORROW DROVE US TO THE NORTHERN WOODS.

BUT OVER THE NORTHERN WATERS PLOWED WITH OTTER,
OVER PONDS, MARSHES, LACUNAE IN COLD GROUND,
OVER THE REFUGE FROM THE TOWNS ONLY WOODSMEN KNOW
ROSE A FLOATING MOVING SOUND,
THE MOCKING CALL OF MELANCHOLIA'S CLOWNS:

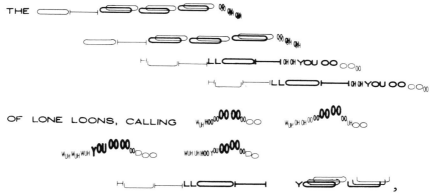

WANDERERS ALONE IN THE NORTHERN GLOOM,

HUNTING IN THE COLD OF THE NORTHERN GLOOM!

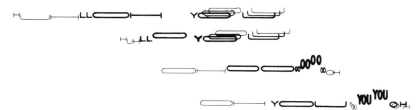

SWALLOWED, BROKEN OFF AS THOUGH SOME LONELY HUMAN

GULPING WATER,

LOSING BUBBLES THROUGH THE BLUE

WERE DROWNING ALL ALONE.

FOLLOWING FROM AUGUST ON THE OVER-PALLS OF CLOUDS ON MOUNTAINS

THROUGH THE AUTUMN RAINS,

THROUGH NOVEMBER'S COLD THROUGH THE NORTHERN SOLSTICE,

FOLLOWING THOSE DARK HOURS,

BORN IN THE STORM, MOVING THROUGH THE GLOOM,

OVER THE FROZEN SNOW,

FLOATING OVER THE FARMLESS MARSHES, OVER THE MOST UNHUMAN GROUNDS,

HOMELESS...., ROADLESS.... HUGE

BLOWN OUT OF THE HOLLOWS OF BRUTES, OUT OF THEIR HOUNDED HEARTS,

AROSE THOSE BROODING, YOWLING TONES,

THOSE LONELY RUTHFUL SOUNDS,

THE OPEN MOUTHED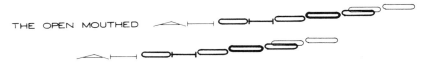

HOWLS OF COYOTES AND WOLVES,

FATHERS OF WARNING, LOW THROATED, CHORDED TO RUMBLE,

NOSE WHOOING TO THE MOON,

NOSE BEADING THE MOON.

BROODING ON THE SLOWNESS, THE LOW PITCH, THE LONG DRAWN TONE

OF THOSE PURSUING VOLUMES OF SOUND

I PONDER WHETHER THEIR SLOW MOTIONS ARE NOT UNCONSCIOUS KNOWLEDGE

HOW OUT OF THE SLOWING DOWN OF ALL MOTION,

OUT OF THE COOLINGS OF SLOWED MOTIONS

GROW THE COLDEST VOLUMES IN THE UNIVERSE....

WHERE ALL POWER IS LOST

AMONG UNKNOWN ZONES OF INSCRUTABLE GLOOM

LOOMING BEYOND THE OUTERMOST STARS,

BOUNDING AN OMINOUS DARKNESS;

AND I WONDER WHETHER THOSE FORLORN CALLS OF THE STORM,

THOSE LONELY CLOUDS OF SOUND

ARE NOT COPYING THE LOWERED TONES OF OUR SORROW

OVER OUR LOSS OF POWER TO THE COLD;

ARE NOT MOCKING OUR MOANS FOR OUR OWN SLOWING-DOWNS

ON GOING ALONE TO THE VOLUME AND HUGE OF ULTIMATE COLD

ON THE SLOW MOTION OF UNBOUNDED AND ALL-ENSHROUDING DARKNESS:

WHETHER THE

CALLS OF THE LOONS,

FORLORN, LONELY, BORN IN THE STORM,

OR THE

HOWLS OF COYOTES AND WOLVES,

OR THE SOUNDS

WOOD WINDS

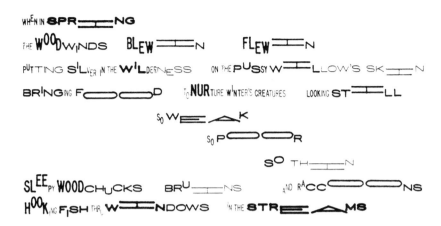

WHEN IN SPRING
THE WOODWINDS BLEW IN FLEW IN
PUTTING SILVER IN THE WILDERNESS   ON THE PUSSY WILLOW'S SKIN
BRINGING FOOD   TO NURTURE WINTER'S CREATURES   LOOKING STILL
SO WEAK
SO POOR
SO THIN
SLEEPY WOODCHUCKS   BRUINS   AND RACCOONS
HOOKING FISH THRU WINDOWS   IN THE STREAMS

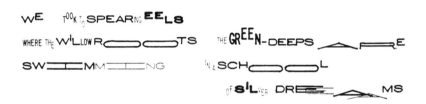

WE TOOK TO SPEARING EELS
WHERE THE WILLOW ROOTS   THE GREEN-DEEPS ARE
SWIMMING   IN A SCHOOL
OF SILVER DREAMS

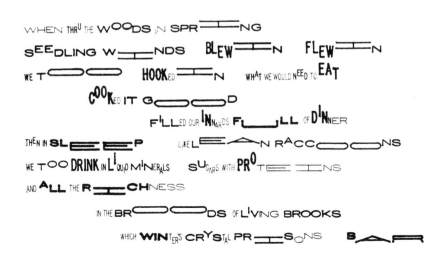

WHEN THRU THE WOODS IN SPRING
SEEDLING WINDS BLEW IN FLEW IN
WE TOO HOOKED IN   WHAT WE WOULD NEED TO EAT
COOKED IT GOOD
FILLED OUR INNARDS FULL OF DINNER
THEN IN SLEEP   LIKE LEAN RACCOONS
WE TOO DRINK IN LIQUID MINERALS   SUGARS WITH PROTEINS
AND ALL THE RICHNESS
IN THE BROODS OF LIVING BROOKS
WHICH WINTER'S CRYSTAL PRISONS BAR

LYRIC FOR A FLUTE

THE LITTLE PEEP, PEEP SEEPS

OF A WINTER CREEK
BENEATH A WOODEN BRIDGE,

BLOWING THROUGH THE WOOD BLUE-PEEPS,

REPEATEDLY REVEALS,

(IN KEEPING UP THESE DRIPS AND LEAKS
OF LITTLE SILVER BIBBLING BEADS)

HOW AERIAL ECHOED SPHERES

COOLY LIFT BALLOONS IN BEATS,

MOVING
        THROUGH THE LONG, LEAN
SEALED-IN-ROOMS OF TUBES,
BOWLS, CLOSED IN CUPOLAS, FLUES,
PIPES, BOOTHS, KEYS, AND FLUTES,

AND THE BLUE WATER BOTTLE OF THE AIR
BETWEEN
        THE LOWERED FLOW OF FREEZING CREEKS

AND THE FROZEN DOME EACH STREAMLET KEEPS
WITH THE CRYSTALLINE EXPANSION
OF ITS ICEN SHEETS.

WITH THE LITTLE PEEP, PEEP, PEEPS,

BOOBLING THROUGH THE WINTER CREEKS,

WE HEAR THE COOL CLEAR TOOTS
IN QUEER KINKED TUNES OF FLUTES,
BLOWING

WITH ACOUSTICAL SIMPLICITY.

THROUGH REEDS WITHIN THE LICKER'S TOOTH

EACH LILLIPUTIAN TUBAL BEAD
LEAPS WITH A CLEAR AND SILVERY SPEED
IN A SERIES OF

FL(oo)-EES   FL(oo)-EES

THESE, PURSUING, PLEA TO YOU AND ME,
(TO BOTH THE OLD AND YOUTH)

WHO WILL **FLEE** WITH ME   WH⊂⊃ ⊂⊃-YOU

WHO WILL DANCE TO THESE COOL TOOTS,

WHO WILL STOOP AND LEAP IN TUNE

WHO **WILL** · · · PLEASE · · · · · WH⊂⊃ ⊂⊃-YOU

WH(oo)-HE   WH(oo)-SHE · · · · · · WH⊂⊃ ⊂⊃-YOU

WHO WILL GO FL(oo)-EE WITH ME

WHO WILL SWING FL(oo)-EE WITH ME

WHO WILL SWING FL(oo)EE FL(oo)EE

WHO SHE WHO HE WHO YOU

WHO WILL SWOOP, THEN KICK?

WHO WILL COAST, THEN FLIT, LOOP AND LEAP
IN HOOPS AND RINGS ON PEAKS OF TOES?

WHO'LL BE TICKLED WITH A QUEER-KINKED TUNE
THOSE TEAK-TIMBERED OVERTONES BALLOON?

WHO WOULD LIMN THEIR AZURE-LOOPED AGILITY
LILTING WITH ATMOSPHERIC ELASTICITY?

T○ WH⟷M·····T○ WH⟷M·····

DO THESE···ₐ═Rⁱᴬᴸᴸʸ BL⟷E

AND FLU'D T⟷NES

BRING B⟷BLING DR═△MS

ₒF **TONE** ᴮᴸₒwₙ **BE'NGS**

BR═△TH═ₙG S○ᴸᵁᴮᴸₑ **IMAGIN**═ₙGS

WHO HEARS IN THESE QUICK DIMPLINGS OF THE WINDS
A WOOING WHISTLING,
EAR-WOOING YOU TO FEEL FLUID
AND FREE
AS THE FLITTERY-MOVING, EVERYWHERE FLUENCIES OF AIR

WHOSE KEYS BEGIN WITH ECHOED PEEP, PEEP, SEEPS,
BENEATH THE ICE ON WINTER CREEKS

AND FINISH WITH THE FLUTE'S QUEER-KINKED TOOTS
AND COOL LIQUIDITIES,

FLITₜₑRING

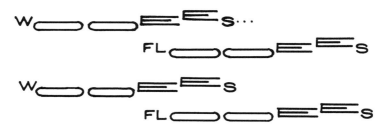

DISCUSSION II

Notation for Phonetic Music
an alphabetic way of writing English prosody

Notation for Phonetic Music
an alphabetic way of writing English prosody

We have discussed notation for phonetic music as an iconistic device where the rise/falls in text look like they sound; where performance and composition modify each other via rehearsals; where memorability of text may be enhanced; and, possibly the most important, where notation becomes a necessary condition in treating the vocal tract as a musical instrument for realizing the tonal messages in contextfree compositions.

Now we wish to consider alphabetic procedures constructed to cue the readers to speak the three dimensions of sound in speech in terms of information potentials, design principles and linguistic values. The last involves a scanning model based on differences in the apparent levels of the three dimensions of sound: fundamental frequency, intensity, and time. This is a broader approach. It includes all the dimensions of prosody, not just the tonal domain of phonetic music.

For simplicity as well as significance we shall reduce this inquiry to two objectives: to write prosodic levels with graphic symbols applicable to many spoken languages and to formulate conversions of prosodic into stress levels. Discussions of the terms "acoustic level," stress level," and "prosodic level" are required for clarification.

Prosody is a vague term. It is associated with systems of versification that may depend on "length" or duration of syllables (Greek),[1] or orderings of weak and strong stressed syllables (English); on rhyme and quasi-rhyme schemes; on stanza arrangements; on relations of syllables to musical notation, etc. All prosodic systems possess two characteristics: they are *written* rhythms of speech and their patterns are *systematic instructions by writers* to readers to speak in specified ways. It is essential to realize that "prosodic levels" must be written. Although every person does hear different levels of loudness or pitch in face-to-face conversation, a continuous symbol system of live speech cannot be fixed or analyzed in detail, or structured or programmed without memory storage of written or other recordings of language. Consequently, prosodic systems connect written and spoken language by graphic cues that identify and program selected units of speech rhythm. We will operate with graphic cues by modifying letters of the alphabet (*Fig. III, P. 83*).

A written prosodic level is a graphic symbol that identifies a perceptible acoustic level and instructs the reader to speak that level. Here, the graphic symbols are elevation, darkness, and length of letter. Since these graphic dimensions are built into the structure of letters, they produce orthographic symbols (*Figs. III and IV, Pp. 83, 84*).

A level is ambiguous without a reference standard. The constant reference for perceiving variations of written prosodic levels is, simply, the normal appearance of letters. It is from this norm that readers judge whether vowels are elevated or lowered; whether all letters are squeezed or stretched out; or noticeably dark or faint. "Normal" appearance is the uniformity of letters consistent with a single style of typography or chirography.

"Acoustic levels" of speech are standard calibrated and instrumentally measured correlates of speech: fundamental frequency in Hz, sound pressure level in dynes, time duration and silences in centiseconds. These energy plateaus and time

FIGURE III.

DURATION

Reduced Vowels	A E I O U THE of
Short	AEIOUWY
Normal	A E I O U W Y
Prolonged	 A E I O U W

SPEECH POWER LEVEL

Quiet unaccented speech (first amplitude level)	A E I O U W Y
Normal conversational level (second amplitude level)	A E I O U W Y
Maximum force and effort (third amplitude level)	A E I O U W Y

FUNDAMENTAL PITCH

Lowest pitch-indicated by depressing the vowels	M$_I$M M$_O$M M$_{AW}$M M$_{EE}$M
Middle pitch-indicated by normal position on line	MIM MOM MAWM MEEM
Highest pitch-indicated by elevating the vowels	M^{I}M M^{O}M M^{AW}M M^{EE}M

CUES FOR VOWEL PITCH MODULATION

Same vowel spoken with rising or falling pitch in periods controllable by speaker

NORMAL SPEED		SLOW SPEED	
RISE	FALL	RISE	FALL

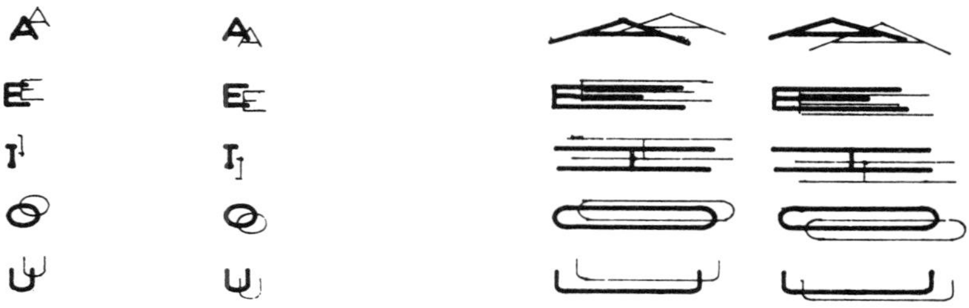

FIGURE III.
Prosodynic code for writing the English alphabet with structured letters that cue the reader to speak the acoustic levels of prosody.

FIGURE IV.

ENGLISH SPELLING

DO NOT ASK WHAT YOUR COUNTRY CAN
DO FOR YOU, ASK WHAT YOU CAN DO
FOR YOUR COUNTRY.

AMPLITUDE

DO NOT **ASK** WHAT **YOUR COUN**TRY CAN
DO FOR **You** ASK WHAT **YOU** CAN DO
FOR YOUR **COUN TRY**

TIME

DO NOT ⟋⟍ SK WHAT YOUR COUNTRY CAN DO FOR YOU
⟋⟍SK WHAT YOU CAN DO FOR YOUR
COUNTRY

PITCH

Do NOT ᴬSK WHAT YOUR COUNTRY
CAN DO FOR YOU ASK WHAT YOU CAN
DO FOR YOUR COUNTRY

AMPLITUDE + TIME + PITCH + PAUSES

FIGURE IV.
Prosodynic cues written separately and combined. Notice the graphic independence of these cues.

dimensions constitute the most universal physical features and coordinates of stress and prosodic levels. The prosodic correlates to acoustic levels are: perceived pitch for fundamental frequency, duration for time, perceived effort and force of speech for amplitude level, and pauses for silences. "Speech power" may be used for convenience, in its loose sense as a perceptual term for "effort and force"; this only for the purpose of instruction to subjects.

A spoken prosodic level is vocalization of a perceived acoustic level in obedience to written instructions. The form of the instruction may be the ∕ ∪ markings of the English departments' "feet" which are simply stressed versus unstressed syllables. Other instructions may be diacritical markings such as Trager and Smith's 1, 2, 3, 4 markings for "pitch" levels, and ∕ ,∧ ,∖ ,∪ for four levels of stress.[2] During the eighteenth and nineteenth centuries prosodic instructions to speak "loudness" levels, pitch levels, time, and pause durations were written with musical notations as in the systems of Joshua Steele and Dr. James Rush.[3] Even though prosodic levels are "naturally" present in face-to-face speech, the vocal performance of prosodic systems as in singing or playing a musical instrument requires training, practice, and no audio-vocal disabilities.

Stress levels are impressions of loudness relative to the average loudness of an individual talker. They are auditory perceptions of undifferentiated vocal energy. It is assumed that native speakers of English who listen, repeatedly, to a single English sentence can identify and specify with markings, three to four levels of stress. The acoustic correlates of stress or loudness include all the acoustic correlates (fundamental frequency, amplitude, and time) of prosodic levels. It is not surprising that listeners will judge the relative loudness of synthesized speech according to the magnitude of the energy levels independent of which acoustic correlate was "traded" or

FIGURE V.

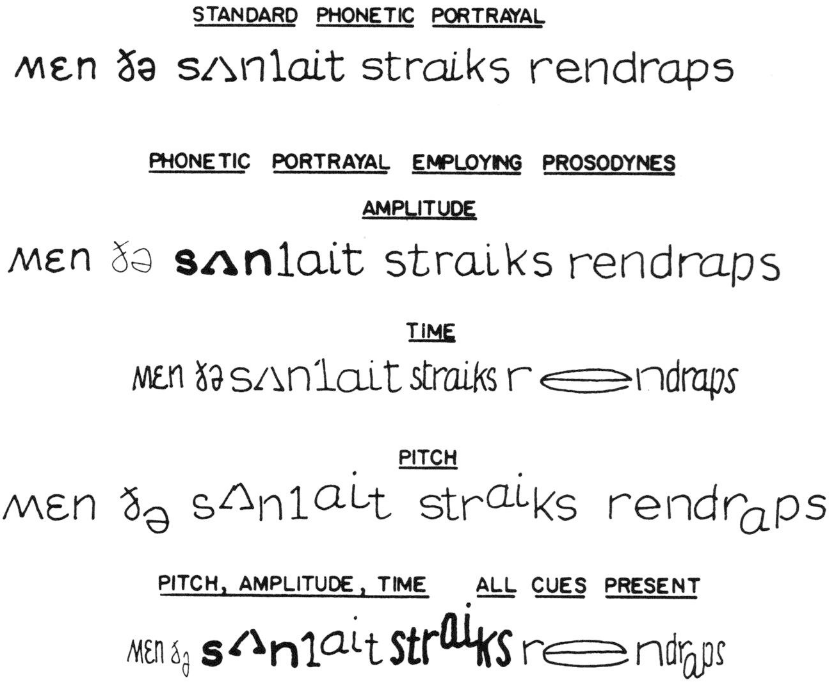

STANDARD PHONETIC PORTRAYAL

ʌɛn ðə sʌnlait straiks rendraps

PHONETIC PORTRAYAL EMPLOYING PROSODYNES

AMPLITUDE

ʌɛn ðə **sʌn**1ait straiks rendraps

TIME

ʌɛn ðə sʌn1ait straiks r⊂⊃ndraps

PITCH

ʌɛn ðə sʌn1ait straiks rendraps

PITCH, AMPLITUDE, TIME   ALL CUES PRESENT

ʌɛn ðə sʌn1ait straiks r⊂⊃ndraps

FIGURE V.
Prosodynic writing of phonetic English. Notice adjustability of the independent dimensions in the prosodynic code to the IPA.

substituted. In correspondence Pierre Delattre has stated, "It is true that amplitude and duration can affect our perception of intonation. (With speech synthesizers I can produce the impression of rises in pitch by over-emphasizing the duration as long as the amplitude is not below normal)." It is the limited information potential of three to four stress levels per syllable in contrast to nine prosodic levels per syllable that indicates the richer speech pattern potential inherent in a prosodynic cue system. This increase of speech information creates problems involved with the capabilities of speakers, the peculiarities of English, the training of speakers, and other questions beyond the scope of this discussion.

Perception of acoustic levels will increase both with their redundancy and in reduced or context free language.[4] Context free English occurs in specialized languages of poetry, advertising, song lyrics, nonsense syllables, short phrases in speech research, short sequences in foreign language teaching, speech therapy, deaf pedagogy, and any isolated short sequence of language of four to five syllables. Over the last forty years instrumental measurements of context reduced language show that listeners can recognize at least three levels of fundamental frequency, three levels of amplitude, and three periods of duration.[5]

The perceived acoustic dimensions and levels of prosody must be recorded in a readable form to be available for use and understanding by speech and language specialists in many areas. If they are presented solely by spectrographic or other instrumental displays, both cost and convenience impose severe limitations. The kind of notation becomes important for teaching and creative uses. Diacritical notations – even when restricted to a few suprasegmentals such as juncture, intonation, and stress – have shown serious deficiencies.[6]

Integrating Prosodic Levels with the English Alphabet

Alphabetic cues which instruct readers to speak prosodic levels specified by the *length, height, and darkness* of letters seem to make several contributions. First, they graphically denote with the same symbol system (letters) all the acoustic dimensions of prosody carried by phonemes, syllables, words, phrases, contours, and sentence envelopes. Secondly, the graphic aspects of the script enable readers to scan stress patterns and visualize acoustic levels. This kind of writing is, literally, a display of transitions from perceived acoustic to stress levels; and the converse. Heights and slopes of levels are essential components of these displays as in spectrographs of fundamental pitch or intonation.[7] A third asset of alphabetic cues is their capacity to show variations of intensity and duration of consonants, variations that modify stress.[8] Fourthly, the change in fundamental frequency of a vowel synchronized with intensity and duration variations can be written as "pitch modulation" cues (*Fig. III*). Fifth, a prosodic expression of the semantic intent of the writer can be written. Alphabetic cues which instruct readers to speak prosodic levels specified by the length, height, and darkness of letters have been called "prosodynes" (*Fig. III, P 83*).[9]

In linguistics the "schwa" is now termed a reduced vowel. When we scan spectrographs, visually, a reduced phoneme appears as a trace. We shall use "reduced" and "trace" interchangeably. The trace warrants special consideration. There is a physical reason for attaching a value of 1 to the reduced vowel or syllable. The reduced vowel is essential in prosody because it operates as a cue for continuity or discontinuity of speech. Its faint and rapid glottal rumble puts sharp dips into the acoustic rhythm of English. Reduction obliterates distinctive features and minimizes the quality in levels of pitch and loudness close to the thresholds of perception (i.e., to no quality). Therefore the trace is allocated no perceived pitch or amplitude values. Yet a reduced vowel exists. It consumes noticeable time. Consequently, the reduced vowel or syllable has been designed to be singular (*Fig. VI*). It is labeled "1" among the numbers given to prosodic levels. This cue is written $A \rightarrow o\ T_1\ P \rightarrow o$ to show pitch and amplitude approaching 0 in perceptive value. The information of the trace plus pitch modulation cues considerably increases the potential of prosodynic print. (*Fig. VI, P. 90*)

Scanning with Prosodynic Levels

A prosodic number is the sum of numbers assigned to each perceived acoustic level of pitch, force, and duration. The largest prosodic number for a vowel equals the sum of the three numbers denoting the highest level of perceived pitch 3, the most powerful amplitude level 3, and the longest time extension 3. The sum is 9. This will be the most stressed vowel or syllable. The smallest sum of level numbers in a vowel will be 1 for the singular trace syllable or vowel. This is the least stressed syllable. The larger the prosodic number, the greater the amount of acoustic energy and stress value *(Fig. VIII, P. 92)*.

Stress levels here are synonymous with "loudness" levels. These levels are functions of objective and subjective components. The objective parameters are three measurable "acoustic levels"; the subjective factors are three prosodic levels, each "a *perceived* acoustic level." Prosodynic levels are both written and spoken. They can be assessed as contributors to "stress" or loudness. It is understood that listeners may concentrate on stress at one time, and on the prosodic levels that produce stress or loudness at another. Targets of attention are involved with training. Although "stress" or "loudness" are produced by many non-acoustic influences, here, on a phonological basis stress is the impression of gross undifferentiated loudness carried by the longitudinal waves of sound. Figure VIII shows how many distributions of prosodic levels may produce the same stress level and why "trading" in prosodic levels occurs.[10] Writers of prosodynic print continuously operate with this kind of trading.

When we scan the speech rhythms of English with these numerical measures, we gain insight by understanding the problems of a writer intent on writing phrases and sentences with prosodynic script. Here is where judgments enter. The maximum number of gross stress levels amounts to 4. It is easier to first select a stress pattern of 4 levels that to first think of 46 prosodic levels. Once the stress pattern is structured, then prosodic levels fall into place.

FIGURE VI.

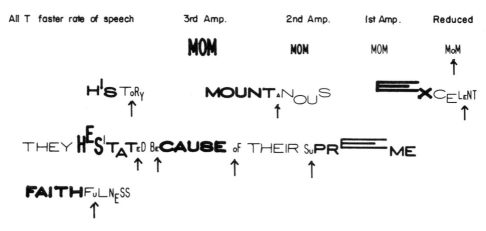

All T faster rate of speech   3rd Amp.   2nd Amp.   1st Amp.   Reduced

FIGURE VI.

The graphic cue for reduced vowels or syllables. Although this "schwa" cue is needed, arithmetically, to specify four stress levels and is a readable cue, speakers seldom articulate a reduced A —o, T_1 P —o vowel differently from an A_1 T_1 P_1. See note under Figure VIII for arithmetical operations that support a value of 1 for reduced vowels.

FIGURE VII.

	Stress Level	Stress Quality	Prosodic Amp. T P Number	Prosodic Quality
▲	1	Minimum Detectability	0 + 1 + 0 = 1	Reduced
C_A^N	1	Inconspicuous	1 + 1 + 1 = 3	Weak
T_E^ST	2	Inconspicuous	1 + 2 + 1 = 4	Weak
B^E	2	Between inconspicuousness and prominence	1 + 1 + 3 = 5	Between Weak and Rich
D^A NCE	3	Prominent	2 + 1 + 3 = 6	Rich
C^O N	3	Prominent	2 + 2 + 3 = 7	Rich
O_NE	4	Most Conspicuous	3 + 2 + 3 = 8	Powerful
W==LD	4	Most Conspicuous	3 + 3 + 3 = 9	Powerful
B=====LL	4	Most Conspicuous	3 + 3 + 3^+ = 9^+	Rich and Powerful

FIGURE VII.

Qualitative associations between numbers of stress levels and numbers of prosodic levels.

90

Arithmetic can convert prosodic into stress levels. We have represented the perceived pitch, amplitude, and time levels by the numbers 1, 2, 3, ranging from small to large. *Then, to determine the stress level of any particular vowel or syllable with respect to its .. neighbor take the difference between the sums of the numbers assigned for pitch, perceived amplitude, or time and divide by two.* Thus a difference of two prosodic numbers on two syllables will give one stress level difference. Since the smallest prosodic number is 1 for the trace and the largest is 9, the highest stress level is $\frac{9-1}{2}$ or 4. In English, 4 has been accepted as a maximum stress level by many workers.[11] Divisions by two are supported by experiments. These show that whenever two prosodic levels of two neighboring syllables – such as pitch and duration, or pitch and perceived amplitude, or perceived amplitude and duration – increase in the same direction, then at least one stress level difference is observed 90% of the time.[12] This stress difference between two syllables implies that levels of their third prosodic dimension remain constant. A graphic portrayal of how differences in prosodic levels within a sentence can generate 4 stress levels is presented in Figure IX., P. 93.

When we deal with prosodic numbers we consider sums of numbers assigned to perceived levels. Prosodic states operate with permutations of these numbers. A prosodic state is any combination of three levels of perceived pitch, amplitude, and time. Since each of these three parameters has three levels, the total of their permutations $=3^3=27$. This applies to all non-modulated prosodic states. The number of modulated states would equal another 27 were it not impossible for the modulated pitch and force effort cues to work in fast time (*Fig. VIII*). With medium and slow durations there are 2 x 3 x 3 = 18 modulated prosodic states (*Fig. VIII*). Add to these unity for the singular reduced vowel. The final sum is 27 + 18 + 1 = 46. Figure VIII also makes it evident that extremely high or low stressed

FIGURE VIII.

PROSODIC FREEDOM OF THE WRITER

n = the sum of numbers assigned to levels of perceived pitch, amplitude and duration. These are prosodic numbers specified for a specific vowel or syllable by the writer.

Column totals = summations of *number of ways* of writing a prosodic number. Each of these permutations may be considered a "prosodic state."

(n=9)	(n=8)	(n=7)	(n=6)	(n=5)	(n=4)	(n=3)
A+P+T	A+P+T	A+P+T	A+P+T	A+P+T	A+P+T	A+P+T
3+3+3	2+3+3	1+3+3	2+2+2	1+3+1	1+1+1	
1	3+2+3	3+1+3	3+2+1	3+1+1	1+1+2	1
	3+3+2	3+3+1	2+3+1	1+1+3	1+2+1	
	3	3+2+2	3+1+2	2+2+1	3	
		2+3+2	1+3+2	2+1+2		
		2+2+3	1+2+3	1+2+2		
		6	2+1+3	6		
			7			

1+3+6+7+6+3+1=27=number of choices for the writer of non-modulated syllables

(n=9)	(n=8)	(n=7)	(n=6)	(n=5)	(n=4)	(n=3)
A+PP+T	A+PP+T	A+PP+T	A+PP+T	A+PP+T	A+PP+T	A+PP+T
3+3 +3	3+3 +2	3+2 +2	3+1 +2	2+1 +2	1+1 +2	Nothing
1	3+2 +3	2+3 +2	2+2 +2	1+2 +2	1	because
	2+3 +3	2+2 +3	1+3 +2	1+1 +3		fast
	3	1+3 +3	2+1 +3	3		duration is
		3+1 +3	1+2 +3			impossible
		5	5			for pitch
						modulation

1+3+5+5+3+1=18=number of choices for the writer of modulated syllables.

Non-modulated states=27
Modulated states   =18
Trace syllable   = 1
46=Total Prosodynic States (choices) per syllable

FIGURE VIII.

"Prosodic freedom" of the writer or the number of choices for writing syllables with different prosodic numbers. The shape of this matrix is somewhat similar to the normal distribution curve. Exercise of this "freedom" is reduced by all the constraints of English except in poetry, language research, and other special uses.

FIGURE IX.

Converting prosodic numbers by difference into relative stress levels for pairs of monosyllabic words in a sentence. Suppose we had no trace value of 1. Then, we could not calculate 4 levels of stress as a maximum difference between a pair of most and least stressed syllables; i.e., $\frac{9-1}{2}=4$. Yet, we know by experiment that 4 levels of stress are perceivable in non-contextual English. This is the rationale for attaching "1" to reduced vowels. It is an arithmetic device for satisfying experimental values.

FIGURE IX.

1.5 Converting Acoustic Numbers by Difference into Relative Stress Levels

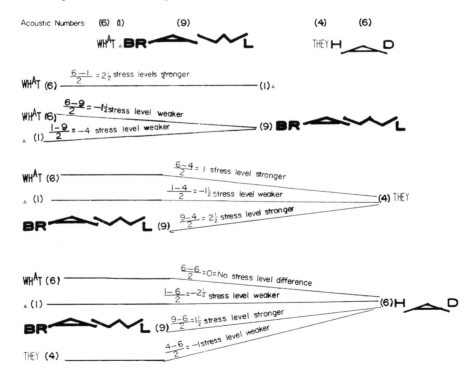

vowels demand the fewest prosodic decisions by the writer while medium stressed vowels maximize the number of decisions.

Discussion of Information in Graphic Design

Prosodynic print carries more of English speech into print than either diacritical marks or standard English orthography. Its information is primarily graphic. One might say that prosodynes are less visible speech than the visible intentions of speech; particularly, the writer's intentions. Because the subjective intentions of the speaker determine emphasis, prominence, and other information of prosody, clarification of a writer's prosodic intention may reveal substantial amounts of information.

When we look at written language from a strictly graphic point of view, the cues of prosodynic print appear to exploit the limits of distortion of a letter without destroying its recognizability. Each variation of shape of a letter may be counted as a choice in the structure of that letter. Accordingly, the number of choices within the limits of recognizability is a kind of "graphic information." It is this sort of graphic information which is the visual essence of these cues.

The print is designed to look as it sounds. This is accomplished by selecting physical features that occur in both the spoken and written symbols of prosody: up-down markings identify up-down pitch; amount of blackness represents amount of vocal force and effort; extensions of length identify extensions of time; blank white space stands for silence of pauses. These associations are structured so that foreign readers may more easily identify the prosody of a second language. This isomorphism can be assessed by comparative tests with diacritical symbols.

Prosodynic dimensions are spatially independent. The occurrence or non-occurrence of one prosodynic cue in no way affects the occurrence of any other cue. As a result displays of a single letter's cues for pitch, apparent amplitude, and time do not interfere with perceptions of contours of intonation or loudness. Spatial independence is an important component of graphic design. Its opposite, conjugality, causes confusion; e.g., when the height dimension of size as a cue for loudness cannot be separated from the elevation of vowels as a cue for pitch in intonation contours.

It is well known that the consonants contribute more than the vowels to our recognition of both aural and written language. This has been shown to be involved in establishing phonetic music. *(P. 13)* The meaning of the sentence below can be read more easily from consonants than from vowels.

E'* *A*I** **I*** *U**E* *I**Y ***EE *O **E*E*A**
SH*'S T*K*NG FL*GHT N*MB*R F*FT* THR** T* CL*V*L*ND

This cue system maintains consonantal intelligibility by keeping consonants on the same line. This uniformity fixes the eye on a graphic standard of reference. Reference standards increase the information of stimuli.[13] It is the vowels that carry most of the information in this system. Here, vowels are the principal cues for pitch because vowel sounds are the prime source of perceptions of frequency and intonation in English.

Prosodynic print instructs readers to articulate consonants with different efforts and durations, along with vowels at varying pitch, intensity, and durations. These orthographic contrasts enable readers to visualize transitions from prosodic levels to stress levels at a glance. Stress patterns are in the orthography.

This study observes at least four criteria for increasing the information of notations, the power of written language symbols where "power" means the number of events a symbol might identify:

1. The smaller the linguistic units, the more information they carry; i.e., alphabets give more information than syllabaries.
2. Spatial independence of cues.
3. Multi-dimensionality in contrast to single dimensional cues.
4. A graphic reference standard for perceptual judgment.

Finally, it should be noted that prosodynic print has been used for speech therapy on two patients[14] and in creative poetry.[15] A better understanding of the basic processes involved and on their application calls for continued testing; e.g., on the model for converting prosodic levels into stress levels.

Summary

An orthographic technique for writing English prosody has been developed by distortions of length of letters, differences in darkness, and the elevations of letters, and by varying extensions of white space between words. The three perceived dimensions of prosody (pitch, apparent amplitude, and time) are *numerically* matched by three *independent* graphic dimensions (elevation, darkness, and length). The independence of the discrete graphic symbols are at least as independent as the symbols in the continuous oral system.

BIBLIOGRAPHY

1. **W. W. GOODWIN & C. P. GULICK. Greek Grammar** (Waltham, Mass., 1958), P. 26. The Greeks attached duration or length to their vowels as a function of the number of consonants that followed the vowel. This was one factor in scanning Greek poetry. Clearly, numerous scanning systems can be written dependent on cue instruction to emphasize this or that cue component of a language.

2. **G. L. TRAGER AND H. L. SMITH. An Outline of English Structure** (Washington, 1957), P. 49.

3. **JOHN WALKER. On Pronunciation of Proper Names** (Philadelphia, 1808), P. 306.
   JOSHUA STEELE. Towards Establishing the Melody and Measure of Speech to be Expressed and Perpetuated by Peculiar Symbols (London, 1781), Pp. 24, 189-190.
   H. A. GLEASON. An Introduction to Descriptive Linguistics, rev. ed. (New York, 1961), P. 45.
   ERNEST M. ROBSON. The Orchestra of the Language (New York, 1959), P. 44.
   DR. JAMES RUSH. Philosophy of the Human Voice, 1855.

4. **NAOM CHOMSKY. Syntactic Structures** (The Hague, 1957), P. 38; note on prosodic compensation in reading "non-grammatical strings."
   PHILLIP LIEBERMAN. Intonation, Perception and Language (Cambridge, Mass., 1967), P. 166. See also reference to "degrees of stress on isolated words," P. 182.

5. At least three levels of perceived pitch (frequently 4 levels) have been observed by many linguists and phoneticians **(LIEBERMAN,** Pp. 171-195). Short duration intervals range from 0.04 sec. to 0.12 sec.; average durations from 0.20 sec. to 0.28 sec.; long durations from 0.40 sec. to 0.48 sec.; SD = 0.041 sec. For measurements of these periods which give a mean ratio 3:1 = long duration/short duration, see reports by:
   G. E. PETERSON & I. LEHISTE. "Duration of Syllable Nuclei in English." **Jrn. Ac. Soc. Amer.,** XXXII, No. 6, 1960, P. 702.
   D. B. FRY. "Duration and Intensity as Physical Correlates of Linguistic Stress." **Jrn. Ac. Soc. Amer.,** XXVII, No. 4, 1955, P. 768.
   J. N. PICKETT & I. POLLACK. "Intelligibility of Excerpts from Fluent Speech." **Lang. and Speech,** VI, 1963, July-Sept., Pp. 156-159.
   GEORGE A. MILLER. Language and Communication (New York, 1951), P. 74.
   A. H. HOUSE. "On Vowel Duration in English." **Jrn. Ac. Soc. Amer.,** XXXIII, 1961, No. 9, Pp. 1174-1178.
   PIERRE DELATTRE. "A Comparison of Syllable Length Conditioning Among Languages." **Sonderdruck aus IRAL,** IV, 3/1966, Pp. 186-196. An amplitude difference of 9db between two syllables in the same linguistic environment equals one loudness level in short English. See the phon scale of loudness level in **HARVEY FLETCHER, Speech and Hearing** (New York, 1958), Pp. 177-194 for tonal loudness levels, and Pp.

76-78 for ranges of speech power over 60db from very quiet to extremely loud speech. This range is broad enough to cover three loudness levels in continuous flow of talk that varies between soft spoken and shouted words. These intensity level differences are standard psycho-acoustic knowledge. That the wide db range of talk does not frequently occur in conversation excludes neither its possible occurrence nor the desirability to be able to identify it by notation.

6. **CLAUDE WISE. Applied Phonetics** (Englewood Cliffs, N.J., 1951), Pp. 182, 397.
PIERRE DELATTRE. *"Comparing the Prosodic Features of English, German, Spanish, and French,"* **Sonderdruck aus IRAL,** Vol. I. 3/1963, P. 194. Delattre has shown, convincingly, the need for graphic representation of suprasegmental information and the inadequacy of numerical identification of levels as vocal instructions. An adequate notation should reach visual-minded people. That this is not a trivial consideration is substantiated by the role of geometry in the history of mathematics: **RAYMOND L. WILDER, Evolution of Mathematical Concepts** (New York, 1968), Pp. 106-109.
RALPH N. HABER. *"How We Remember What We See,"* **Scientific American,** 5/1970, Pp. 104-112.

7. **ILSE LEHISTE & GORDON PETERSON.** *"Some Basic Considerations in the Analysis of Intonation,"* **Jrn. Ac. Soc. Amer.,** XXXII, No. 4, 1960, Pp. 451-454.
FRY. Pp. 765-768.
A. E. ROSENBERG. *"Effect of Pitch Averaging on the Quality of Natural Vowels,"* **Jrn. Ac. Soc.Amer.,** XLIV, No. 6, 12/1961, Pp. 1593-1594.

8. **PIERRE DELATTRE.** *"A Comparison of Syllable Length Conditioning Among Languages,"* **Sonderdruck aus IRAL,** IV, 3/1966, Pp. 186-196.
P. DENES. *"On Statistics of Spoken English,"* **Jrn. Ac.Soc. Amer.,** XXXV, No. 6/1963, P. 898.

9. Originally prosodynes were presented to the Phonetics, Linguistic, and Voice Science Interest Group in New York City at the December, 1965 meeting of the SAA, under the name of *"Intonemes".* In 1967 **PIERRE DELATTRE** wrote a letter suggesting the term "prosodeme". I modified "prosodeme" to "prosodyne" because of the association of energy with "dyne" and energy levels of prosody.

10. **PHILIP LIEBERMAN.** *"Some Acoustic Correlates of Word Stress in American English,"* **Jrn. Ac. Soc. Amer.,** XXXII, No. 4, 1960, Pp. 451-454.
FRY. Pp. 765-768.

11. **G. L. TRAGER & H. L. SMITH. Outline of English** (Norman, Oklahoma, 1951). Daniel Jones has specified several stress levels for "sense groups" of short English; only two stress levels for long conversation. Evidently, Philip Lieberman agrees with Jones (**Intonation, Perception and Language,** P. 182). Further support of three to four stress levels in short English comes indirectly from the need to specify six different db levels on the newer sonograph displays of speech spectrographs. The classic loudness scales

(Fletcher, Stevens, Garner) also suggest three to four levels of "loudness" as range limits.

12. LIEBERMAN. Pp. 453-458; **FRY.** P. 767.

13. I. POLLACK. *"Information of Elementary Auditory Displays,"* **Jrn. Ac. Soc. Amer.,** XXV, July, 1953, Pp. 765-769.

14. *"Intonemic Orthography in Speech Therapy"* presented April, 1967 to the Pennsylvania Speech and Hearing Association conference in Pittsburgh. Therapy was conducted by Anne Highland at the Speech and Hearing Clinic, University of Pennsylvania Hospital, Philadelphia.

15. ERNEST M. ROBSON. Transwhichics (Chester Springs, Pa., 1970).

DISCUSSION III

Formant Music
in
Vowel and Diphthong Tones

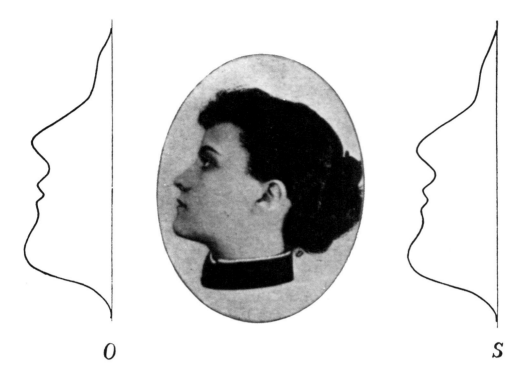

O S

Reproduction of a portrait profile by harmonic analysis and synthesis.

Curve is as follows, the numerical values corresponding to a wave length of 400:

$$
\begin{aligned}
y = \ & 49.6 \sin (& \theta + 302°) & +17.4 \sin (2 \, \theta + 298°) \\
+\ & 13.8 \sin (3 \, \theta + 195°) & + 7.1 \sin (4 \, \theta + 215°) \\
+\ & 4.5 \sin (5 \, \theta + 80°) & + 0.6 \sin (6 \, \theta + 171°) \\
+\ & 2.7 \sin (7 \, \theta + 34°) & + 0.6 \sin (8 \, \theta + 242°) \\
+\ & 1.6 \sin (9 \, \theta + 331°) & + 1.3 \sin (10 \, \theta + 208°) \\
+\ & 0.3 \sin (11 \, \theta + 89°) & + 0.5 \sin (12 \, \theta + 229°) \\
+\ & 0.7 \sin (13 \, \theta + 103°) & + 0.3 \sin (14 \, \theta + 305°) \\
+\ & 0.4 \sin (15 \, \theta + 169°) & + 0.5 \sin (16 \, \theta + 230°) \\
+\ & 0.5 \sin (17 \, \theta + 207°) & + 0.4 \sin (18 \, \theta + 64°).
\end{aligned}
$$

This equation was set up on the synthesizer, and the portrait, as drawn by the machine, is shown above.

FROM: DAYTON CLARENCE MILLER, 1916

Discussion III is a technical presentation of the principles underlying formant music.

Historically some poets sensed intuitively, and groped for formant music.

What is formant music? Circa 1845-1846 Edgar Allen Poe presented the *Music of Poetry* as the end for which "the soul.... when inspired by the poetic sentiment struggles... the creation of supernal beauty. Its sole arbiter is taste." He carried this concept further in his *Philosophy of Composition*.[1] There Poe analyzed his most popular poem *The Raven* as a controlled rationale that fabricated his composition as though it were a machine to produce *intended effects* on an audience. In his expliqué Poe claimed he selected "Nevermore" and, of course, "Lenore" because "these considerations led me to the long /o/ as the most *sonorous* vowel in connection with /r/." Later Pallas was selected, partly, "for sonorousness" of vowel quality.

The poet of adolescent genius, Arthur Rimbaud, perceived by ear what is called today "vowel coloring" although *not* with Rimbaud's categories. His statement published in 1873 follows: "I invented the color of the vowels: A black, E white, I red, O blue, U green; I regulated the form and movement of each consonant, and, with instinctive rhythms, I prided myself in inventing a poetic language accessible some day to all the senses. I reserve translation rights."[2]

Sidney Lanier, in 1880 published *The Science of English Verse*. Here he showed familiarity with works of sound by the physicists Wheatstone and Helmholtz. He knew music. These backgrounds combined to produce a system of versification. Unfortunately, Lanier did not understand the acoustic parameters of speech in contrast to song and, especially, in contrast to instrumental music.[3]

Lanier's contention that rhythms of poetry, song, and instrumental music are all functions of time is correct but they are by no means identical in the physical character of their sounds, in metric precision and form, or in acoustical range. Nor do they relate in the same semantic ways to natural and artificial languages.

Since there was very little laboratory data to answer these questions before 1916, and little until 1947 (*Visible Speech* publication), and much more between 1947-1977 one can only commend Poe, Rimbaud, and Lanier for asking the right questions. . . . prematurely.[4]

The first version of the formant music presented here was researched and written 1938-1941. Over the more than four decades since 1938 it has been used and revised and in 1956 was recognized.[5] It originated as one of several answers to the question: What are the materials, the physical tools of the writer? This is a materialist approach.

Another influence, structural, and truly an inspirational one, came from Dayton Clarence Miller's book, *The Science of Musical Sounds*, 1916. Miller conceived of translating a woman's profile into music via trigonometric curves. His statement was: "If mentality, beauty and other characteristics can be considered as represented in a profile portrait, then it may be said that they are also expressed in the equation of the profile. . . In this sense beauty of form may be likened to beauty of tone color, that is to the beauty of a certain harmonious blending of sounds." *(See P. 102 for portrait and equations)*

Given these harmonious curves for music, what shapes may they assume with the sounds of speech in poetry? From then on I took the long journey to understand the sound imagery of poetry; its audibility for readers and listeners; its intelligibility; its powers of expression; the foundation of poetry as a lyric art.

The formant music I shall present includes three components:

1. a coupling of dominant and recessive vowel resonances;
2. placing a diphthong next to vowels that carry the resonances of the diphthong. These are imperceptibly fused formants which make a diphthong be a singular sound, a phoneme. They are recessive, i.e., we do not hear them as isolated tones;
3. pairings of dissonant vowels.

Throughout Discussion I we have noted the acoustic nature of formants, their physiological location, their uniquely human features and their manifestation in the vowel whisper tone scale. *(P. 16)* Here we shall present the spectrographic information and frequency relations that determine formant music. There are four formants of which two are the most powerful and by far the most influential on our hearing. They are designated F_1 and F_2 and identify the lowest and next to lowest resonances of a vowel during speech. Formants 1 and 2 will be written F_1 and F_2. Below is a graph of F_1 and F_2 formants for the vowel ah (α).

FIGURE X.

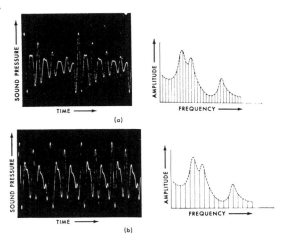

The wave shapes and corresponding spectra (formants) of the vowel "ah" pronounced (a) with the vocal tract frequency of 90Hz, (b) with 150Hz. Notice the constant shape of the "ah" formant in spite of the different vocal chord frequencies.

P. B. DENES AND E. N. PINSON 1963

105

FIGURE XI.

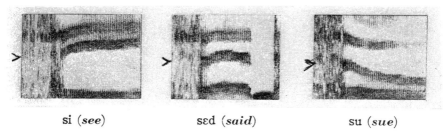

si *(see)*   sɛd *(said)*   su *(sue)*

Notice different heights of F₂ frequencies for different vowels. (see arrows)

FROM: *VISIBLE SPEECH,* POTTER, KOPP AND GREEN 1947

Between 1938-1941 I ordered the vowels on the basis of the perceived heights of their tones. In 1950 I tested and revised the slope of whispered vowels. The rising pitch of this scale[4,7] is most easily observed if the reader will whisper aloud: moot, mote, mutt, mat, mate, meet. Whispers give steadier states than voicing by eliminating fluctuations of fundamental pitches from the larynx and pharynx. (See P. 16 for vowel scale). The frequency range of any person's formants frequently varies only 2½% to 4%. This is involuntary. The voluntary range of the fundamental frequency of speech varies between 20% and 100% depending on dialect, the individual's octave, and training of his/her voice.[28]

The "tones" in the whisper scale are produced solely by formants. Below is a series of the formants of vowels with a white line drawn through those levels that determine the slope of audible whispered pitches. Notice how that line runs through F_1.

FIGURE XII.

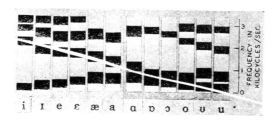

R. POTTER AND G. PETERSON 1948

the lowest formant of low back vowels, then runs through the midway region (between F_1 and F_2) of the middle vowels, and finally, rising, passes through the second formant and only the second formant of the front vowels. The line of descending or ascending pitch of vowel formants told me that F_1 of all the vowels could *not* fit the slope of the pitch scale; neither could F_2. Through the lowest sections F_1 dominates while in the highest section F_2 dominates the perceptions of heights of whisper pitches; in the middle vowels pitch is a blend of both F_1 and F_2.[8] *Accordingly, a dominant formant may be defined as the formant which determines a vowel's position on the whisper tone scale.* But what about the other major formant of a vowel that does not fit into the whisper tone scale? That formant I called "recessive". In this way the vowel scale influenced me to conceive of dominant and recessive tones as everpresent components of every vowel. Now no writer can write or hear an isolated formant in natural speech. But writers can arrange vowels to carry patterns of dominant and recessive formants. A poet can pair up vowels that share formants in the same frequency region or couple vowels that share recessive overtones, also *in the same frequency region.*[10] It was these observations that led me to develop formant and diphthong music. *(Figs. XII, XIII)*

FIGURE XIII.

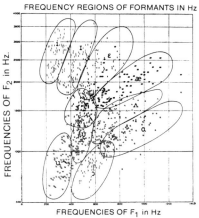

FREQUENCY REGIONS OF FORMANTS IN Hz

FREQUENCIES OF F_2 in Hz.

FREQUENCIES OF F_1 in Hz

FIG. XIII. Frequency of second formant versus frequency of first formant for ten vowels by 76 speakers.

G. PETERSON AND H. BARNEY 1952

Before presenting melodious pairs of vowels, a word of caution. Just because you can hear a whisper tone scale determined by formants does not mean that you are hearing isolated formants. We are only hearing dominant frequency *levels* of quite complex tones.

Formant regions are *frequency areas* determined by vocal cavity resonances. *(Fig. XIII)* Although these frequency regions vary trivially for successive articulations of the same isolated vowel by the same person they do vary considerably with their phonetic contexts, their stress, and with extreme differences in fundamental pitch. That is why the influences of consonantal levels are important for the poet to control.[9] *(Fig. XIV)*

FIGURE XIV.

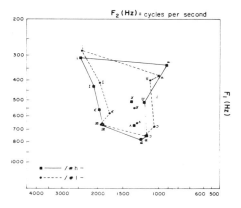

FIG. XIV.   Average values of F_1 versus F_2 for the 10 vowels excerpted from the neutral context (h. .d) and from initial / ɪ / context.

Z. B. BOND   1976

Variations of formant region due to sex, age, or dialect, are far greater than variations within the individual's speech. Yet vowels spoken by different age, sex, and dialect groups are recognizable. The multiple relations that support vowel recognition in spite of these variations will not be discussed here.[10, 16] What pairs of vowels do share a resonant region and how do they sound and how have they been used? One such couple is /oo/ as in cool vs. /ee/ as in eve. The *dominant F_1 region* of /oo/ is the same as the recessive *F_1 region* of /ee/. *(See Tables A, P. 109 and G_1, P. 122)* If the reader will whisper and then speak: Lucille, Louise, Looreen, Jean Boone, Lee Bloom, Lou Lee. . . . some of the melody in lifting vowel overtones above subliminal hearing may be sensed and felt. The vowel tone music in [oo ⟷ ee], doubly underlined below, is quite evident in that most famous lyric in the popular show *No, No, Nannette.*

"Picture you upon my knee
Just tea for two and two for tea
Just me for you and you for me alone."

Notice how the last syllable "lone" is musically contrapuntal and dramatically contrastive as it should be.

TABLE A

Frequency Levels in Hz.

VOWEL	DOMINANT	RECESSIVE
oo in boot (u)	F_1 375 ←	F_2 825
ee in meet (i)	F_2 2500	F_1 → 360

A second pair of vowels sharing dominant/recessive overtones are: [ŏŏ in wood (ʊ) ⟷ ĭ in hit (I)]. The regions overlap, but are not as identical in frequency areas as [oo ⟷ ee]. *(Table A).* The dominant is /ŏŏ/, recessive is /ĭ/. We may hear the surfacing of this subthreshold melody in: Cindy Wood, Cyril Loofkin, Willy Wolf, spring woods, wood winds, Pussy Hoodwin.

A composition whose acoustic undercoating includes both [oo ⟷ ee] and [i ⟷ oo] is titled *Wood Winds.*[11] It commences:

When in spring
the Wood Winds blew in, flew in
blew through, flew through,
putting silver in the wilderness
on the pussy willow's skin;
bringing food to nurture winter's creatures
looking still
So weak
So poor
So thin.....

Complete Composition on P. 75.

TABLE B

Frequency Levels in Hz.

VOWEL	DOMINANT	RECESSIVE
aw in all (ɒ)	F_1 625	F_2 850
ĕ in bed (ɛ)	F_2 1900	F_1 610

A third couple is aw in all / ɒ / vs. ĕ in bed / ɛ /, again a dominant overtone F_2 in / ɛ /. Some harmonious blends of vowels are audible in "and forget this lost Lenore... nevermore, nevermore," substantiating Poe's argument for sonorousness in the refrain of his poem, *The Raven.* This melodiousness may be heard by whispering and speaking other words besides Lenore, i.e., Glenn Fall, Nell Shorn, Saul Shell, Dell More, Paul Cornell, Maude Bellemore. *(See Table B)*

We now observe two more pairs of vowels that share formants; and both are couplings with /oo/. They are: [oo ⟷ aw] and [oo ⟷ ah].

TABLE C

Frequency Levels in Hz.

VOWEL	DOMINANT		RECESSIVE	
oo in boot (ʌʌ)	F_1	375	$F_2 \rightarrow$ 825 ←	
*ah in father (ɑ)	F_1	800 ←	F_2 1250	
aw in all (ɔ)	F_1	625	F_2 850 ←	

*See Note under Table G_1, P. 122.

One may hear these overtones surface through the choral refrain (written in orthography designed by the author to represent the intensity, frequency, and duration changes in speech intended by the poet). See below.

An example in recent sound poetry of the [aw ←→ oo] euphony occurs in David Roth's minimal composition of pitch variations, alternating tempos and intensities within the phrase *Water For You*[12]

I WATER FOR YO⊂⊃⌐⌐⌐

II WATER FOR YOU   WATER FOR YOU
(whispered)

III WᴬTER FₒR YOU ˙YOU YOU YOU

We hear [ah ←→ oo] or [oo ←→ aw] in Yale's "Boolah" song and in Paul Shoom, Norma Loon, Ahbdoolah, John Woo, Lou Dawn. A phrase that combines [ĭ ←→ oo] with [oo ←→ aw] occurs in: "in the music, the calling. . . . in wolves forlorn moon songs." That we can write different vowel pairs with several tonal values in a single line is worth attention. Allowing a ten vowel or ten syllable sequence to a line, it is possible to write five vowel couples (each reversibly) in 252 different ways. Combining all couples in four successive lines gives 252^4. This puts few constraints on acoustic patterns for speech composers.

The dominant/recessive concept led me to diphthong music.

Diphthongs are glides of F_2 regions that blend with such a rapid rate of frequency change that we hear the diphthong as a single sound, a phoneme. We may perceive the component F_2 tones by listening for *the vowels that carry* those *regions* when, and only when, we continuously slow down the *rate of articulation of the diphthong* until its frequency transitions can be noticed. This phonemic decomposition may be reversed by starting slowly with the vowel carriers of the F_2 overtones of a specific diphthong and then speeding the *rate of articulation* until the diphthong is heard. The reader is requested to whisper the diphthong /ow/ as in 'cow', then slow the rate of articulation until the vowels [ah ⟷ o͝o or oo] are identified. The first part of the diphthong is the /ah/ sound in 'hot' and the last sound either that in 'wood' or in 'moon'. The /o͝o/ and /oo/ terminations depend on the individual's personal dialect, sometimes on regional dialect. The same procedure should be followed with the diphthong /oh/ to make [oh = o ⟶ o͝o or oo]. We shall now present the 6 diphthongs with their quite different *rates of transitional* F_2 regions.

TABLE D

DIPHTHONGS WITH DIFFERENT RATES OF TRANSITION IN THEIR DECISIVE F_2 REGIONS (Hz mille-sec).
THESE F_2 REGIONS ARE SHARED BY VOWELS. P. 113

TABLE D

	RATE	F$_2$ CHANGE (Hz /msec.)
	slow	5.7
oy in boy (ɔi)	moderate	5.3
	fast	5.8
	slow	3.4
ī in bite (αɪ̆)	moderate	3.7
	fast	3.8
	slow	1.3
ow in howl (au)	moderate	1.1
	fast	1.1
	slow	0.5
oh in go (o)	moderate	0.3
	fast	0.1

THOMAS GAY "*LANGUAGE AND SPEECH*" 4-6/1970
Vol. 13, P. 86

Data from Thomas Gay's table tell why we started with /ow/ and /oh/. Their rates of F$_2$ frequency changes are the slowest and therefore the easiest to decompose for perception. It may be remarked in passing that Thomas Gay's syntheses of diphthongs from played back recordings of their frequency regions (with hearing tests) contributed the most information to this analysis. Models for synthetic drawings of F$_2$ regions are developed from spectrographs of diphthongs, similar to those which appear below.[17] The reader should realize that the visible speech of spectrographs is *not* visible hearing.[16] The sound poet should consider speech spectroscopy with respect – and a large grain of salt. What is inaudible is useless to the speech composer.

FIGURE XV.

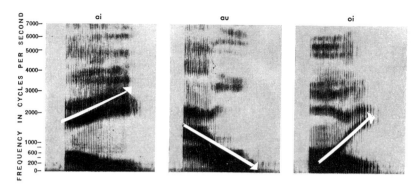

P. B. DENES AND E. N. PINSON 1963

You see from Fig. XV that diphthongs besides being imperceptibly fused by rapid rates of F_2 overtone transitions, are also characterized by differences in direction. Some diphthong glides rise in frequency; others fall. Following are tabulations of the rising, then falling diphthongs.

TABLE E

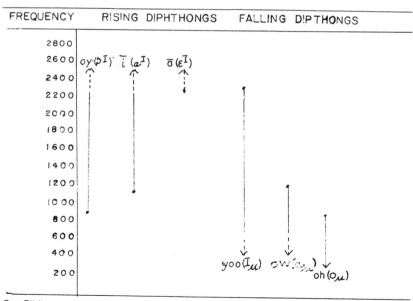

See Bibliography, #'s 10, 13, 14, 17, 18, 19.

The reader should now decompose aloud or compose these diphthongs via slowed rates of whispering or speech. Because of their faster rates of F_2 fusion, some diphthongs are more difficult to decompose or compose: oy (ɔ̝); i (aI). *(See Table D, P. 113)*

Table E *(P.114)* also shows that frequency ranges of diphthong glides as well as their up or down directions and their rates of articulatory transition distinguishes one diphthong from another. A speech poet may exploit these differences.

Since I'm not aware of other poets who composed by coupling diphthongs with vowels that carry their recessive F_2 regions I will present two samples from my own poetry. These compositions were written in 1941-1942, therefore this question is warranted: the most precise diphthong measurements were conducted in 1962-1970 so how could I have composed with these pairs 20 years before 1962?[14] The answer is in the exercises I have proposed. These oral/aural variations in speeds of speech enabled me to detect traces of vowels and initial and terminal vowel sounds in diphthongs *by my own vocal syntheses...* whispered and spoken. Although I did not fully understand the parameters involved until Thomas Gay's paper, I was able to write diphthong compositions with vowel components that carried the F_2 region in the diphthong glide; and to hear these glide-hidden tones come to life in tonal poetry. As shown in the opening movement of *The Dirge of the Cold* considerable redundancy was needed to establish diphthong music with [ow = ah ⟶ oh ⟶ o͝o . . . oo], the acoustic theme. *(P. 72)* Observe the contrapuntal value of high vowels in the line, "the kinked complaints of metals on the streets. *(P. 72)* The uses of energy levels in the acoustics of this composition interested me and are discussed elsewhere.[11]

Redundancy is not the only way to enhance the recessive tones in the neighborhood of a diphthong. The rise or fall of the recessive F_2 tones may be written to move in the same direction as the rising or falling order of the F_2 regions that dominate the glide. These ascensions or descendings of formant frequencies create scale-like tones that suggest the latent pitch curve in the diphthong's glide. The diphthong [ã = ĕ --> ĭ . . . ee] governs the sound pattern of the following lines:

> "Elfin faces wet with rain
> Singing in emerald hills
> In rhythm with self-centered spins
> Of strange terrains."

Besides redundancies and slopes another way to enhance audibility of recessive F_2 regions in glides is to flank them with consonants and *semi-vowels that sustain the same F_2 levels.* This technique allows a freer, wider set of choices than rime, yet it achieves the original purpose of rime: to stabilize adjacent vowel tones. These tonal techniques do not impose on the poet the semantic inhibitions of rime. Certain consonants may sustain the high /ee/ in niece, teach, sieze, cheat, tease, each, seen, cease; and others may lower the /ee/ frequency with consonants/semi-vowels in meal, fear, veal, leave, veer. Tables G_4 (P. 124), G_5 (P. 125) show the effects of consonants on adjacent vowels.

Other studies reveal that vowels located in a consonantal context are more recognizable than isolated vowels; vowels imbedded in words are more identifiable than isolated vowels.[9] This acoustic information tells sound poets and other speech composers: minimal phonemic compositions of vowel and consonant structure will be more perceptible with occasional use of syllables and words than isolated phonemes. Likewise, melodic themes borne by phonemes may be clarified or enhanced even by infrequent occurrences of syllables and words.

Another diphthong composition is *The Voice of the Buoys*.[11]
Here diphthong / $\bar{\iota}$ / in bite and /oy/ in boy appear with their
gliding recessives: [$\bar{\iota}$ = ah $\longrightarrow$ ($\bar{a}$) $\longrightarrow \iota$ or ee] and [oy =
aw $\longrightarrow$ (uh or $\bar{a}$) $\longrightarrow \breve{\iota}$ or ee] when spoken slowly. Due to the
acoustic prominence of their wide ranging glides, their long
duration, and the intrinsic powers of their initiators, /ah/ and
/aw/, these diphthongs are among the loudest of phonemes.
Consequently, this poem may be, inherently, one of the loudest
in English. Here, too, the loudness supports and is supported by
the theme.

> The tonged recoils of the noise of the buoys,
> Drawn with the long clong that iron hawsers haul
> Are always calling,
> Always calling,
> How this rising-falling
> Stays stably based upon an unchanged origin,
> Beneath the sweeps.
> It seems to be a lean and mineral tree
> Recoiling from the buoyant whorls of salty water
> In dawns beneath the sea;

Complete Composition on Pp. 68-70.

The consonants marked for their pitch influence and the set
of 6 diphthongs with the vowels carrying the F_2 regions of their
glides are presented in the complete tabulation of this tonal
system. *(Table G_5, P. 125)*

The conclusion of this speech music is the set of dissonant
vowel couples. *(Table G_3, P. 123)*

My original method for determining pairs of dissonant
vowels was to factor the dominant formants of nine vowels: ee
/ ι /, $\breve{\iota}$ /I/, e / ε /, $\breve{a}$ / $\mathfrak{X}$ /, ah / a /, ŭ / Λ /, aw / $\mathfrak{I}$ /, oo / U /,
oo / μ /, and six diphthongs: $\bar{\iota}$ / a^I /, oy / $\mathfrak{I}^I$ /, $\bar{a}$ / ε^I /, oh

/O ʊ /, yoo /I ʊ /, ow /a ʊ /. When no numerical values appeared that yielded ratios or a highest common multiple or anywhere near to any integral values these pairs were interpreted as dissonant. Twenty-nine years later three of four of my dissonant pairs were shown by controlled experimentation with 300 listeners to include the four most powerful masking agents among vowels in this order: ĕ / ε /, ă / æ /, aw / ɒ /, oo / ʊ /.[15] *(Figure XVI below)*

FIGURE XVI.

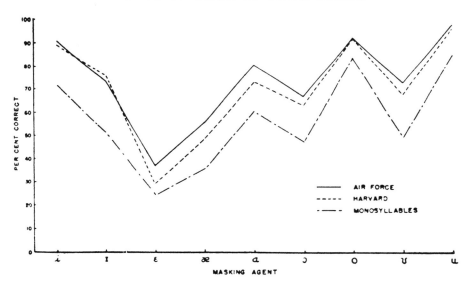

Fig. XVI. Articulation scores of spondees and monosyllables masked by nine prolonged vowels.

J. J. O'NEILL AND J. J. DREHER 1958

Two sounds tend to mask each other when they occupy the same frequency regions. A lower frequency neighbor tends to mask a higher one. The three pairs of masking prone vowels given are characterized by most powerful energy levels between 700 Hz and 1000 Hz. They appear in the dissonant composition, *17 Noises in the Testicles of an Old Giant.* Notice how a title may lend sense to apparent gibberish and how orthography can clarify the acoustic intent of the poet's performance. *(See P. 33)*

Following the principle that similar dominant frequency regions tend to mask each other, particularly when the lower comes *after* the higher frequency tone, a fourth dissonant pair is included: [ŭ in sun (**⋀**) ⟷ ŏŏ in wood (**ᴜ**)] i.e., bum goods, tough crooks, fun books, Bud Zooks, dumb looks. In these pairs the inherent phonetic power of /ŭ/ is greater than /ŏŏ/ so the former may mask the latter just as well as in reverse order: hood mugs, cook guts, Zook Rudd, good grubs.

Another dissonant composition built with the same three pairs of garbage sounding vowels as in *17 Noises* follows. But this time syntactical and meaningful sentences carry the dominant patterns and give semantic reinforcement to these patterns. *(See "Crows", P. 71)*

At this point the reader may ask "Why all this association of dissonance with masking?" The reasoning, subject to tests independent of my compositions, takes this track. The infliction of noise and/or confusion on auditory perception is a discomfort. A state of uncomfortable perception can be contrastive with melodious vowel sequences whether in pairs of isolated vowels or in adjacent syllables or words. In passing, the importance of consonantal selection for writing dissonant pairs of syllables is difficult to overemphasize. The number, the noisiness, and the intrinsic amplitude of consonants will surely determine the dissonant powers of syllables or words. *(Table G₄)* Noisy consonants are: *ks, tch, rk, dj, lk, lch, g ʒ , r ʒ , rf, mz.* Composers of sound poetry can only enrich their work by paying attention to this kind of acoustic information.

The reader may also wonder: how can identical frequency regions in a vowel pair at one time cause dissonance, another time melody? Answer: when the most powerful, *dominant* regions of two vowels are shared the result is dissonance; when one or two recessive tones are shared, then the effect tends to be melodious. The greater the distance in frequency between dominant formants, the clearer the vowel differences in tone. This is illustrated by Table F, P. 120.

TABLE F

DISTANCES BETWEEN MEDIAN FREQUECIES OF DOMINANT FORMANTS OF 76 SPEAKERS, MALE, FEMALE AND CHILDREN (See Fig. XIII, P.   , BARNEY AND PETERSON 1952)

SONOROUS PAIRS	SEPARATIONS IN Hz
$(\iota)_{F_2}$ —— $(\mu)_{F_1}$	2380
$(I)_{F_2}$ —— $(\upsilon)_{F_1}$	1825
$(\varepsilon)_{F_2}$ —— $(\jmath)_{F_1}$	1310
$(a)_{F_2}$ —— $(\mu)_{F_1}$	805
$(\jmath)_{F_2}$ —— $(\mu)_{F_1}$	220

Subscripts designate the dominant formant

ah (α) values half way between F_1 and F_2.

aw ($\jmath$) and oo (μ) share their recessive F_2 regions yet they are clearly sonorous because their all important and powerful F_1 regions are sufficiently separated to avoid masking. The couple $\breve{a}$ in cat ($æ$): ah (α) have been omitted even though they share their recessive F_2 regions. Their F_1 regions are close to 700 CPS. . . a masking condition.

These pairs of sonorous and dissonant vowels complete my tonal techniques for writing speech music. Summations of these acoustic procedures for reference by sound poets, prosodists, and/or linguistic students appear on Tables G_1, G_2, G_3, G_4, G_5. They also should be of considerable interest to writers of radio and TV texts, songwriters and librettists.

Discussion

In 1941 an early version of formant music was called "vowel harmonics." During February 1942 a paper on this subject was submitted for publication to the Acoustical Society of America via J. B. Kelly, then one of the higher placed engineers and editors at the Bell Telephone Laboratories. Kelly thought there would be interest in the paper for Acoustical Society members but little likelihood they could apply, practically, the principles underlying the approach. He also raised the question whether the use of these principles would effect improvement in composition. The answer: new procedures with a repertoire of more numerous sounds, as in the use of the Moog synthesizer, do *not* guarantee excellence or creativity. But new acoustic information does guarantee an increased potential for an acoustic art... even though the art (here poetry) is not exclusively acoustic. Given two sound poets with identical abilities except for their repertoire of speech sounds, surely the one with the richer acoustic pallette can create more interesting compositions.

Kelly's other objection, that he saw no applicability of the ideas presented for the acoustic society members, was the usual objection to cross disciplinary work. What interested me then, and still does, is the helplessness of the cross disciplinary worker in the hungry world of institutional specialization... this in spite of the lip service paid to cross disciplinary values... a situation still current. The solution may be reached through organized support for experimental research to increase the information and/or the power of symbols in the arts.

We shall now present a summation of dominant/recessive formants in pairs: diphthongs with their imperceptible F_2 vowel regions; the dissonant vowel pairs, and sets of consonants and semi-vowels marked for their influences on the pitch of adjacent vowels. This tabulation includes all components of this speech music.

FINAL TABLE

TABLE G₁
PAIRS OF VOWELS SHARING FORMANTS THAT PRODUCE MELODIOUS TONES

VOWELS		DOMINANT		RECESSIVE	
oo in boot (u)	F_1	375	F_2	825
oǒ in wood (ʋ)	F_1	475	F_2	1200
aw in all (ɔ)	F_1	625	F_2	850
ǔ in sun (ʌ)	*F_1	700	F_2	1400
ah in father (a)	*F_1	800	F_2	1250
ǎ in cat (æ)	⊘F_2	1750	F_1	835
ě in bed (ɛ)	F_2	1900	F_1	610
ĭ in hid (I)	F_2	2200	F_1	460
ee in meet (ι)	F_2	2500	F_1	360

* middle vowels with median frequency areas higher than F_1; /ah/ and /ǔ/ are on approximately the same level of pitch on the vowel scale. *See Fig. I, P. 16.*

ǎ or (æ) is so irregular in its frequency areas that it ambiguates rather than integrates tonal perceptions with one exception: when close to oo or ee.

The data in this table has been influenced by careful measurements of 100 speakers of different sexes and ages by four Bell Laboratory workers, and others.

TABLE G₂

DIPHTHONGS AS INDEPENDENT PHONEMES WITH THEIR TRANSIENT F₂ VOWEL REGIONS

RISING DIPHTHONGS

	INITIAL	MID COURSE	TERMINAL
oy in boy =	aw (ɔ) ⟶	ǔ (ʌ), ā (ɛᴵ) ⟶	ĭ (I), ee (ι) when slow
ī in bite =	ah (a) ⟶	ā in ate (ɛᴵ) ⟶	ĭ (I), ee (ι) when slow
ā in ate =	ě (ɛ) ⟶	none ⟶	ĭ (I)

FALLING DIPHTHONGS

	INITIAL	MID COURSE	TERMINAL
ow in howl =	ah (a) ⟶	aw (ɔ), oh (oʋ) ⟶	oǒ (ʋ), oo (u) when slow
oh in go =	oh (o) ⟶	none ⟶	oǒ (ʋ), oo (u) when slow
yoo in few =	ī (I) ⟶	none ⟶	oǒ (ʋ), oo (u) when slow

TABLE G₃

DISSONANT PAIRS OF VOWELS

ă in   cat(æ) ⟷ aw in caught(ɔ)
ĕ in   red(ɛ) ⟷ ă in rat(æ)
o͝o in wood(ʊ) ⟶ oh in road(oʊ)
ŭ in   sun(ʌ) ⟶ o͝o in stood(ʊ)

Note on G_1, P. 122.

G. M. Kuhn of the Haskins Laboratory published a report, Jrn. Ac. Soc. Amer., Vol. 58, No. 2, 8/75, showing that perception of "front cavity resonance" enables F_2 levels to contribute their dominant higher frequency information. This is consistent with relations presented in Table G_1. Only in the case of ee / i / does F_3 become significant; and that does not destroy the dominant/ recessive relation with oo / u /. Kuhn's spectrographs in normal speech of back vowels indicate higher F_1 peak amplitudes than their F_2 components. These values tend to support the dominant/recessive concept of this system. Kuhn's fricational spectrographs also support the elevation of F_2 frequencies by fricatives presented in Table G_5, P. 125. See highest tone words and syllables.

TEST TABLE FOR INFLUENCES

Test Table For Influences
of Consonants on Formant Levels of Adjacent Vowels.

v=vowel	High Vowels				Mid Vowels		Low Vowels		
No Pitch	(i) ee	(ɪ) ĭ	(ɛ) ĕ	(æ) ă	(a) ah	(ʌ) u	(ɔ) aw	(ʊ) oo	(u) oo
h+v									
k+v									
v+k									
k+v+k									
High Pitch									
ch+v									
v+ch									
ch+v+ch									
sh+v									
v+sh									
s+v									
v+s									
Low Pitch									
m+v									
v+m									
m+v+m									
l+v									
v+l									
l+v+l									
f+v									
v+f									
f+v+f									
p+v									
v+p									
p+v+p									
b+v									
v+b									
b+v+b									
*V+v									
v+V									
V+v+V									

*V = V used as a consonant

TABLE G₅.   TONAL MATRIX

TONE LEVELS OF PHONEMES
(formant determined)

EFFECTS ON PITCH LEVELS

CONSONANTS

HIGH

- S in hiss (S)
- Sh in dash (Ŝ)
- T in tot (T)
- Ch in each (tŜ)
- Y in you (Y)
- N in pin (N)
- D in bid (D)
- Z in fizz (Z)
- ʒ in azure (ʒ)
- J in judge (dʒ)

NEUTRAL
Little effect on pitch levels

- Ng in sing (ŋ)
- Th in thin (θ)
- H in he (H)
- K in kid (K)
- G in gut (G)
- Dth in they (ð)

LOW

- P in pool (P)
- R in rear (R)
- M in me (M)
- B in boy (B)
- F in off (F)
- V in over (V)
- W in leeward (W)
- L in kill (L)

HIGH VOWELS and DIPHTHONGS

| ee (iː) | i (ɪ) | a (eɪ) | e (ɛ) | a (æ) |
| meet | hid | die | bed | cat |

HIGHEST TONE WORDS / HIGHEST AND TONE SYLLABLES

MIDDLE VOWELS and DIPHTHONGS

| u (ʌ) | ah (ɑ) | i (aɪ) | oy (ɔɪ) | u (uː) |
| sun | father | bite | boy | few |

MIDDLE TONE WORDS / MIDDLE AND TONE SYLLABLES

LOW VOWELS and DIPHTHONGS

| ow (aʊ) | aw (ɔ) | oh (o) | oo (ʊ) | oo (uː) |
| howl | all | go | wood | boot |

LOWEST TONE WORDS / LOWEST AND TONE SYLLABLES

NOTES:
D indicates Diphthongs; ↑ or ↓ their up or down motion.
Subscripts 1,2, indicates pre or post vowel consonants.
Voiced consonants tend to be lower in pitch levels than their unvoiced counterparts.
L_1 may initiate with its upswing of the tongue a lilting effect such as in lyric, leap, lilt, light; W_1 as in wine, wit, wing, wed.

125

BIBLIOGRAPHY

1. **EDGAR ALLEN POE, The Complete Works of Edgar Allen Poe, Including Essays on Poetry,** ed. J. H. Ingram (The Home Library, A. L. Burt Co., N.Y. circa 1874)

2. **FORLEY, WALLACE,** *Rimbaud* (University of Chicago Press, 1975, Pp. 121, 193)

3. **SIDNEY LANIER, Centennial Edition of the Works of Sidney Lanier,** ed. Charles R. Anderson (John Hopkins Press, 1945)

4. **POTTER, KOPP AND GREEN,** *Visible Speech* (D. Van Nostrand Co., N.Y. 1947)

5. **SCHLAUCH, MARGARET, Modern English and American Poetry** (Watts, London, 1956) Pp. 171-174, unpub. manuscript, **"Vowel Harmonics",** 1941. See discussion by J. B. Kelly, P. 121.

6. **CRANDALL, I., The Sounds of Speech,** Bell Telephone Technical Publication 11/1925 – Reprint B-162-1

7. **ROBSON, E. M., The Orchestra of the Language** (A. S. Barnes & Co., Cranbury, N.J. 1959) Pp. 50-62

8. **MORTON, J. AND CARPENTER, ALAN,** *Experiments Relating to the Perception of Formants,* **Jrn. Ac. Soc. Am.,** Vol. 35, 4/1963, P. 475

9. **BOND, Z. B.,** *Identification of Vowels Excerpted From /L/ and /R/ Contexts,* **Jrn. Ac. Soc. Am.,** Vol. 60, No. 4, 10/1976 P. 906

10. **PETERSON, G. AND BARNEY, H.,** *Control Methods Used in Study of Vowels,* **Jrn. Ac. Soc. Am.,** Vol. 24, No. 2, 3/1952, P. 175. A must for those who wish to understand formant music.

11. **ROBSON, E., Transwhichics,** (Dufour Editions, Chester Springs, Pa. 1970)

12. **ROTH, D.,** *Water For You,* Temple University, Speech Composition, 1975, Unpubl.

13. **GRAY, T.,** *A Perceptual Study of American English Diphthongs,* **Language and Speech,** Vol. 13, Part 2, 4-6/1970. The most thorough and intelligent study I could find on this subject.

14. **LEHISTE, I. AND PETERSON, G.,** *Transitions, Glides and Diphthongs,* **Jrn. Ac. Soc. Am.,** Vol. 33, 3/1961, P. 268.

15. **O'NEILL, J. J. AND DREHER, J. J.,** *Masking of English Words by Prolonged Vowel Sounds,* **Jrn. Ac. Soc. Am.,** Vol. 30, No. 6, 6/1958 P. 539

16. **SCOTT, BRIAN L.,** *Temporal Factors in Vowel Perception,* **Jrn. Ac. Soc. Am.,** Vol. 60, No. 6, 12/1976 P. 1354. Important evidence why visible speech is not visible hearing. A correction on overvaluation of spectrographic information.

17. **P. B. DENES AND E. N. PINSON, The Speech Chain,** Bell Laboratory Educational Publication, 1963

18. R. K. POTTER AND G. E. PETERSON, *The Representation of Vowels and Their Movements*, **Bell Telephone Monograph,** B-1576, 1948

19. THOMAS, I. B., *Perceived Pitch of Whispered Vowels*, **Jrn. Ac. Soc. Am.,** Vol. 46, No. 2, Part 2, 8/1969 P. 469

20. RISMA, R. J. AND ENGEL, F. L., Jrn. Ac. Soc. Am., Vol. 36, 9/1964, P. 1637. Shows perception of complex tones dependent on distance between peak frequencies, i.e., vowels.

21. C. F. SACCIA AND I. R. CRANDELL, *A Dynamic Study of Vowel Sounds*, **Bell Telephone Technical Journal,** Vol. IV, 10/1925, P. 586

22. MILLER, D. C., The Science of Musical Sounds (New York 1916)

23. EPPLER, W. MEYER, *Realization of Prosodic Features in Whispered Speech,* **Jrn. Ac. Soc. Am.,** Vol. 29, 1957, P. 104

24. von HELMHOLTZ, H. L. F., On Sensations of Tone, (Dover Publications, N.Y. 1954) Pp. 108-110

25. H. FLETCHER, *Physical Characteristics of Speech and Music,* **Bell Telephone Publication,** 7/1931 Monograph B-568

26. LENZ, H., The Physical Basis of Rime, (Stanford University Press 1931)

27. PAGET, R. A. S., SIR, The Nature of Human Speech, 1925; **Babel,** 1930; **Human Speech,** 1930

28. My own tests of a five subject group in 1950 with *controlled phonetic environments* were guided by spectrographic information in *Visible Speech,* Potter, Kopp and Green. The first 1939-1941 work on this system utilized data from Dayton Clarence Miller, Sir Richard Paget, and Bell Laboratory workers C. F. Saccia, C. J. Beck, J. C. Steinberg and particularly I. Crandall. An abbreviated form of the 1950 test is shown in Table G_4.